SOVEREIGN

The Life and Reign of Emperor Nicholas II

No. 13   2024

1868   1918

PAUL GILBERT

SOVEREIGN

No. 13

2024

The Life and Reign of
Emperor Nicholas II

ISBN: 9798327872776

Researched from Russian media
and archival sources by
Paul Gilbert

Edited by Paul Gilbert

E-mail:
royalrussia@yahoo.com

BLOG
tsarnicholas.org

Follow me on Facebook:
https://www.facebook.com/royalrussia

Dedicated to clearing the name of Russia's much slandered

FROM THE DESK OF PAUL GILBERT

Dear Sovereign Reader

It is with great pleasure, that I present the No. 13 Summer 2024 issue of *Sovereign: The Life and Reign of Emperor Nicholas II*. In this issue, I present 20 articles about Russia's last Tsar, his family, the Romanov dynasty and the history of Imperial Russia. These articles are based on new research from Russian archival and media sources. Many of them have been published on my blog and are now available in a printed format for the first time. I do this in an effort to preserve my many years of dedication and hard work. I have taken the liberty of updating many of these articles with new facts and photos. In addition, this issue includes new works translated from Russian, and published in English for the first time.

I have been researching and writing about these topics for more than 30 years, and during that time made 29 visits to Russia, which included St. Petersburg, Tsarskoye Selo, Moscow, Ekaterinburg and Crimea. It was during these visits that I met historians, authors, museum and palace curators, among many other interesting persons. Over the years, they have welcomed me during my visits to Russia, and shared their knowledge and archives with me .

Since October 2018, I have focused my resources on clearing the name of Russia's much slandered Tsar. I have been able to achieve this through the publication of my books and periodicals - including the revival of *Sovereign* earlier this year; the organization of the 1st International Nicholas II Conference held in England - and a second in the planning stages; a Facebook page dedicated to Nicholas II with more than 8,000 followers and my popular blog *Nicholas II. Emper. Tsar. Saint.*, which was launched 5 years ago, and has received more than 1 million hits! To date, it features nearly 800 articles and 1000s of vintage and contemporary photographs.

Thank you, dear reader, for your continued interest and support of my research and dedication to clearing the name of Russia's much slandered Tsar.

PAUL GILBERT
1st July 2024

P.S. The iconic image depicted on the cover of this issue is one of a series taken at the Stavka military headquarters at Mogilev in 1915, by one of Nicholas II's daughters.

SOVEREIGN No. 13 2024 · TABLE OF CONTENTS

Imperial Yacht *Standart*:
Nicholas II's palace on the sea

by Paul Gilbert

Elegant style yachts were once the norm among many of the world's most important rulers. The British, the Royal Houses of Europe, and even the Americans have all at one time or another provided their leaders with beautifully appointed yachts that served for both recreational as well as official purposes. But few of these highly specialized ships can compare with the Imperial Yacht Standart, reserved exclusively for the use of Russia's last emperor Nicholas II.

This handsome "ship of state" was a graceful sea-going vessel and was considered the most perfect ship of her type in the world. She was named after the famous frigate of Peter the Great, launched in 1703. Built to the Tsar's own specifications, she was constructed in Copenhagen in 1895 by the Danish firm Burmeister-Wain. The shipyard still maintains a thriving existence but the plans no longer exist for the Standart due to the destruction of the shipyard brought on by two world wars.

Across the North Sea, however, a copy of the plans for the former Imperial Yacht are held in the archives of the National Maritime Museum in Greenwich, England. After a visit to Cowes, the future King Edward VII asked for the plans of the Standart. The plans had been preserved in 1895 by the Admiralty Office when plans for a new British royal yacht were under construction.

The Standart was a superb, black-hulled 5557-ton yacht measuring 401 feet in length and 50 feet wide, making it the largest private ship in the world. She was much larger and faster than that of the other Imperial Yacht's, the Alexandria and the

Polar Star reaching speeds of up to 21.18 knots. Anchored in a Baltic cove or tied up at Yalta, the Standart was as big as a small cruiser. She had been designed with the graceful majesty of a great sailing ship. She combined elegance and comfort and met all the requirements of a floating palace. A large gilded bowsprit in the shape of a double-headed eagle, lunged forward from her bow and three tall masts towered above her two white funnels. White canvas awnings stretched over smooth decks shielding the passengers from the sun, while informal wicker furniture on the main deck invited relaxation. Also on the main deck was a large dining saloon that could seat up to seventy-two guests at one long table for luncheon or dinner.

Below deck was found a formal reception salon and drawing rooms panelled in mahogany, polished floors, brass and elegantly hung crystal chandeliers and velvet drapes. The Imperial Yacht even had its own chapel for the private use of the Imperial Family.

The Tsar's Private Study was furnished in dark leather and simple wooden furniture. The Tsarina's drawing room and boudoir were done in her favourite English chintz. On the walls could be found the indispensible icons or "windows to heaven" along with many photographs of her relatives and family.

Today there are hundreds of photographs in exis-

A magnificent giled bowsprint in the shape of a double-headed eagle lunged forward from the bow of the Imperial Yacht *Standart*

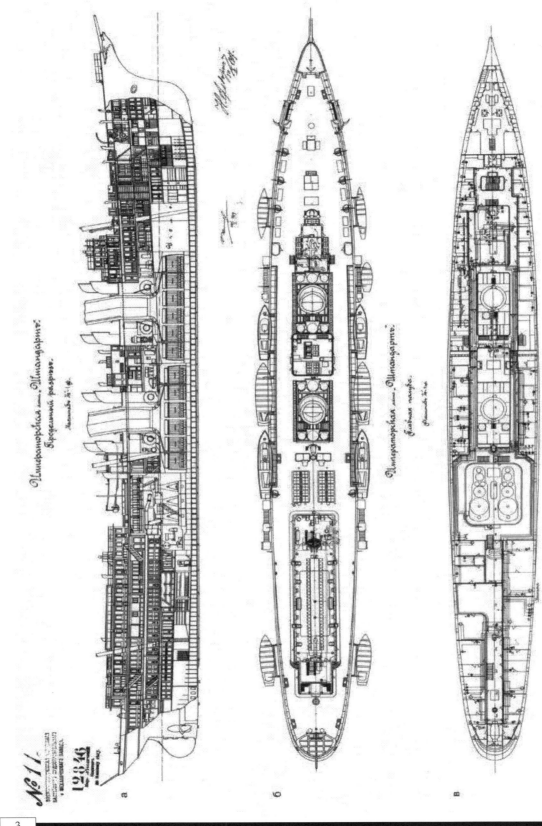

Plans of the Imperial Yacht *Standart* (partial view)

tence of the Standart taken by the Tsar and his family, their relatives and aides, whom at the time were making the most of the latest craze of Russia's upper classes–photography.

Many of these photographs were family photos and never meant for public viewing. They were stuck neatly in old family albums and memory books. Since the fall of the Soviet Union in 1991, hundreds of these "windows on the past" have been published in handsome coffee-table books. To date, the most luxurious of these books has to be Русские императорские яхты каталог 17-20 век (Russian Imperial Yachts: 17th-20th Century) containing nearly 400 photographs [published in 1997, this Russian language book is now out of print].

Among these "pioneer" photographers was General Count Alexander Grabbe, who was often asked to accompany the Imperial Family when they sailed on the Standart to the Crimea and the islands of the Finnish archipelago. A selection of his photographs of the Imperial Yacht were published in 1984 by his son Paul Grabbe in The Private World of the Last Tsar: The Photographs and Notes of General Count Alexander Grabbe. A keen photographer, Grabbe's photographs show the Tsar and his family onboard the Standart as a happy and carefree family, relaxing, playing games, dining with royalty, roller-skating and dancing.

Just before sailing and prior to the arrival of the Imperial Family, the ship was polished and cleaned from top to bottom. Sailors busied themselves above and below deck, checking the lifeboats and adjusting the awnings on the main deck. Officers and crew assembled on deck, all of whom saluted the Tsar as he came on board.

On the Standart, Tsar Nicholas II followed a daily routine. Early each morning he came on deck to check the weather. He also liked to make the rounds of the ship's company as well as greet the Imperial Yacht's warrant officers. It was not uncommon to see the young Tsesarevich Alexis, wearing a sailor's uniform, accompany his father during these rounds. The Tsar was interested in navigation and he liked to discuss this subject with his Flag Captain, Admiral Nikov or as well as checking the yacht's course with Captain Zelenetsky. The Tsar worked for two days each week while at sea, receiving and sending dispatches by the courier boats that arrived daily from the mainland.

When the Standart sailed, she was a glorious and spirited vessel and she attracted attention wherever she went. When the Tsar and his family were on board, a large household staff of footmen, stewards, butlers and cooks attended to their every need, in total she carried a crew of 275. The yacht was manned by a crew from the Russian Imperial Navy. Also on board was a platoon of marines as well as a brass band and a balalaika orchestra. In order to communicate with the mainland and other ships of the Russian Imperal Navy, the Standart was also equipped with radio, a novelty in 1912.

"This relationship of the Imperial Family to its entourage was very friendly and informal," Count Grabbe recalls. "They were especially cordial with the officers of the Standart. These young men were exemplary–charming, modest, possessed of a great deal of dignity and tact, and incapable of intrigue."

The yacht was commanded by Rear-Admiral Lomen, who was responsible for the safety of the Tsar from the moment Nicholas II set foot on board any vessel, whether a yacht, a dreadnought

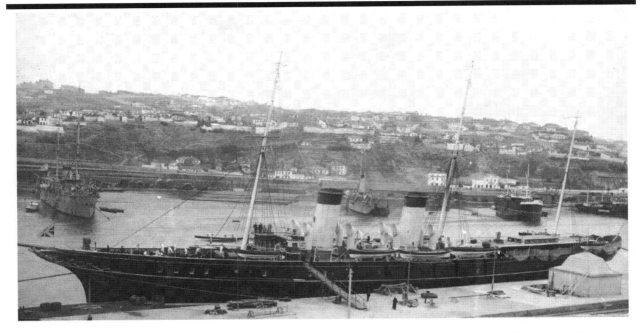

The Imperial Yacht *Standart*, docked in Sevastopol, Crimea. During their visits to Crimea, the Imperial Family often travelled from St. Petersburg on the Imperial Train to Sevastopol, where they boarded the *Standart*, and sailed along the southern Crimean coast to Yalta.

The Imperial Yacht *Standart*, arriving in Yalta, Crimea. The arrival of the Imperial Yacht generated much excitement among the city's residents, many of whom gathered at the pier to get a glimpse of the Tsar.

or a launch. "The whole of the naval administration stood in mortal fear of the Admiral," recalls A. A. Mossolov. "It is true that he asked a great deal, and if he was annoyed he could be extremely rude. He claimed that onboard the yacht the Tsar himself was under his orders! Off duty he was pleasant and sociable."

The actual Commanding Officer of the Standart was Captain Tchaguin, and the second in command, Commander Nikolai Sablin. Both had the satisfaction of being thought of very highly by Their Majesties. In the letters which she wrote to the Tsar when he was at General Headquarters, the Tsarina frequently mentions Sablin.

Life at sea seemed to bring the best out in all the members of the Imperial Family. A.A. Mossolov recalls in his memoirs, "The Empress herself grew gay and communicative onboard the Standart. She joined in the children's games, and had long talks with the officers."

The officers were certainly in an exceptional situation. Almost daily, the Tsar invited these officers to dinner and after the meal liked to play billiards with them or enjoy a game of dominoes. In return the Imperial Family accepted invitations to tea in the mess. On such occasions the Empress usually sat nearby, sewing, the Tsesarevich ran about with his playmates, while the Grand Duchesses, surrounded by all the young men, scattered throughout the yacht. "We form a united family," the Empress used to remark on these memorable and happy voyages."

The family vacations to the Crimea and their cruises on the Standart were a welcome change for the children in particular.

When the Imperial Family went onboard the Stan-

dart, each of the five children was assigned a diadka, a sailor charged to watch over the the child's personal safety. The children played with these diadkas, played tricks on the them and teased them. Gradually the young officers of the Standart joined in the children's games. As the Grand Duchesses grew older, the games changed into a series of flirtations, all very innocent of course. "I do not, of course, use the word 'flirtation' quite in the ordinary sense of the term," remarks Mossolov, "the young officers could better be compared with the pages or squires of dames of the Middle Ages. Many a time the whole of the young people dashed past me, but I never heard the slightest word suggestive of the modern flirtation." Moreover, the whole of these officers were polished to perfection by one of their superiors, who was regarded as the Empress's squire of dames. As for the Grand Duchesses, even when the two eldest had grown up into real women, one might hear them taking like little girls of ten and twelve.

"The girls loved the sea," Count Grabbe comments, "and I well remember their joyful anticipation of these cruises on the Standart, which opened broader horizons for them, brought them new contacts, and permitted an intimacy that was other wise impossible. To be at sea with their father–that was what constituted their happiness."

The Tsesarevich Alexis also loved the excursions on the Standart as well. He enjoyed accompanying the Tsar while he carried out his duties on board the Imperial Yacht. He loved to play games such as shuffleboard. On sunny afternoons it was not uncommon to find an exhausted Alexis stretched out and fast asleep under one of the many lifeboats on the main deck. At times, his haemophilia restricted his movements severely and photographs show the young Tsesarevich walking with the aid of a

A rare photo of the *Standart* (right) moored along the embankment on the Neva in St. Petersburg

Officers transport Empress Alexandra Feodorovna and her daughter Grand Duchess Anastasia to the Imperial Yacht *Standart*. Finnish Skerries, September 1907 or 1908

cane. Due to his illness, a favourite sailor was assigned to watch over Alexis. At first it was the sailor Andrei Derevenko who for some time was patient and conscientious in watching over his Imperial charge; his behaviour toward Alexis, however, became excessively mean after the Revolution. Fortunately, the Tsesarevich also had another sailor-attendant–the loyal Klimenty Nagorny. This sailor was later killed by the revolutionary army that overran Russia after World War I.

So it was, that when the warm months of the summer rolled around that the Tsar and his family set sail on the Standart for their vacation off the coast of southern Finland. For the Tsar, there was no greater relaxation than these restful, seaborne excursions on his beloved Standart. Here his family and found a secluded bay surrounded by small islands where they could relax and enjoy their time together away from the palaces and rigid rules that governed the Russian court. This charming spot was such a favourite of Nicholas II and his family, that they returned to it every year and the children even nicknamed it the "Bay of Standart."

While anchored in the bay, the Imperial Family lived on board the Standart but every day they would get into small launches and head for their chosen island. The island was uninhabited, which offered them complete freedom to picnic, relax, and enjoy the out-of-doors without fear of being observed by prying eyes. It was also on this little island that a tennis court was built for the Imperial Family, tennis being a favourite of the entire Imperial household.

In 1907, an unfortunate incident took place that was later known as "the wreck of the Standart." The incident occurred on a fine day in the Finnish fjords when all of a sudden the Imperial yacht was shaken by a jolt at a moment when there was not

the slightest reason for expecting anything of the sort. Immediately afterwards the yacht was heeled over. It was impossible to tell what might be coming next. The Empress rushed over to her children. She found them all expect the Tsesarevich, who was nowhere to be seen. The anguish of the two parents may only be imagined; they were both beside themselves. It proved impossible to move the yacht. Motor-boats started off towards her from every direction.

The Emperor hurried up and down the yacht, and gave the order for everybody to go in search of the Tsesarevich. It was only after some time that he was discovered safe and sound. At the first alarm his diadka, Derevenko, took him in his arms and very sensibly rushed to the "hawse-pipes," since they offered the best chance of saving the boy if the vessel should be a total loss.

The panic subsided, and all onboard descended into the boats. An inquiry followed. The whole responsibility fell on the pilot, an old Finnish sea-dog, who was in charge of the navigation of the vessel at the moment of the disaster. Charts were hurriedly consulted and showed beyond any possible question that the rock on which the yacht had grounded was entirely uncharted.

There remained His Majesty's Flag Captain, who was responsible in principle for the safety of the Imperial Family. At the time of the accident the post was held by Admiral Nilov, the only master, under God, of the fate of the yacht.

He was in such a state of mind after the accident that the Tsar felt bound to go to him in his cabin. Entering without knocking, the Tsar saw the Admiral bending over a chart, with a revolver in his hand. The Emperor tried to calm him. He reminded the Admiral that under naval regulations he would

Emperor Nicholas II, on the bridge of the Imperial Yacht *Standart*. Crimea 1912

The Imperial yacht *Standart* with illuminations at night in Riga harbour, 1910

have to go before a court of inquiry, but, the Tsar added, there could be not a shadow of doubt that he would be acquitted, for the accident was entirely unforeseeable. The Tsar carried away the Admiral's revolver.

"There was an immediate conspiracy of silence at Court about the wreck of the Standart, recalls Mossolov. "Everybody knew that the slightest criticism of the officers of the yacht would have brought down punishment on the head of anyone who ventured to utter it."

"The officers were chosen for special gifts; their task was to create an atmosphere of a fairytale, a charming idyll. It may be that in technical knowledge they were not absolutely up-to-date."

Many a royal personage was made welcome on board the Standart, including Queen Alexandra, sister of the Dowager Empress Marie, accompanied by her husband, King Edward VII, King Gustav of Sweden and Kaiser Wilhelm II of Germany.

Despite the relaxed atmosphere of the excursions on the Standart, the safety and protection of the Imperial Family was still a top priority. The Tsar was so fearful of assassination that he had several cruisers accompany the yachts at all times. A warning, published in a Finnish newspaper in 1911, reads as follows;

"Notice to all mariners concerning seafaring regulations when the Russian Imperial Yacht is in Finnish waters: Fire will be opened on all commercial shipping and all yachts–whether motor, sail or steam-that approach the line of guard ships. All ships wishing to put to sea must seek permission not less than six hours in advance. Between sundown and sunrise, all ships underway may expect to be fired upon."

Early in June 1914, as usual at this time of the year, the Tsar and his family went on a voyage to the Finnish fjords. The weather was hot, and stifling heat was interspersed with pouring rain. This year, Tsar Nicholas II was not to enjoy the picturesque landscape and relax with the serene joys of family life; since the end of June one piece of bad news had followed another. The assassination of the Austrian Archduke Francis Ferdinand–whom Nicholas and Alexandra had known very well–and the attempt on the life of Rasputin, disrupted the mental equilibrium of the Imperial couple. Within weeks, war was declared and the Standart, by order of the Tsar was placed in dry-dock, and he never again returned to the tranquility of the Finnish or Crimean coastline's.

After the Revolution, the former Imperial Yacht was destined to be stripped of all its former elegance. In 1917, the Standart was renamed Vosemnadtsate Martza. In 1932, she was renamed Marti. Between 1932 and 1936, she was refitted as a drab, grey minelayer at the Marti Yard in Leningrad for service in the Soviet Navy. The heavy gun armament was fitted, as were mine rails. There were 4 rails on the mine deck, and 2 more on the upper deck. The mine deck could carry 580 mines, and 200 could be accommodated on the upper deck.

With the German invasion of Russia, the Marti laid some 3159 mines, and bombarded shore positions near Leningrad. On 23rd September 1941, Marti was damaged in an air attack at Kronstadt, but was quickly repaired to resume action on the 26th of the same month. In autumn 1941, some of her guns were used ashore at Leningrad.

After the war, Marti was refitted and converted to a training ship, renamed Oka. During the refit, the steam engines were replaced by diesels. She was scrapped at Tallinn in Estonia in 1963.

View of the Imperial Yachts *Polar Star* (left) and *Standart* (right), docked at Libau (renamed Liepāja in 1920), located on the Baltic Sea. August 1903. The *Polar Star* and *Standart* are easily distinguished from one another by their funnels and the double-headed eagle figurehead, located on the bow of each vessel. The two funnels of the *Polar Star* funnels are closer together, whereas those of the *Standart* are placed wider apart. The magnificent carved double-headed eagle figurehead of the *Standart* is much more elaborate than that of the *Polar Star*.

Model of the Imperial Yacht *Standart*, from the Collection of the Central Naval Museum in St. Petersburg.

In happier days, Emperor Nicholas II on the deck of the Imperial Yacht *Standart*

The former Imperial Yacht *Standart* refitted for wartime use during the Soviet years

The Soviet Navy's use of the Imperial Yacht *Standart* during the Great Patriotic War

by Paul Gilbert

It seems that royal yachts are today a thing of the past. In the Russian Empire, the last was the Imperial Yacht *Standart* of Emperor Nicholas II. A magnificent ship that survived its owner by more than 40 years and left it's mark on Russia's nautical history.

Why was it renamed several times? Why was the luxury yacht converted into a warship? What combat missions did she perform during the Great Patriotic War? And why did Stalin dislike this ship?

Competition between two emperors

The history of the Imperial Yacht *Standart* began in Denmark at the Burmeister and Vine shipyard. On 29th August 1893, Alexander III, together with Em-

press Maria Fedorovna and Tsesarevich Nicholas Alexandrovich [future Emperor Nicholas II], arrived on the Imperial Yacht *Polar Star* in Copenhagen, where the Emperor ordered the construction of the new ship.

"There was an unspoken competition between Emperor Alexander III and Emperor Wilhelm II of Germany. When Wilhelm built himself the ocean yacht *Hohenzollern*, Alexander III decided to outdo him with an even more splendid vessel," claims the Russian marine writer Vladimir Shigin.

On 1st November [O.S. 20 October] 1894, Alexander III died. The sovereign never stepped on board the new yacht, however, he did manage to give her a name in honour of the first ship of the Russian fleet, and the beloved frigate[1] of his ancestor Peter the Great. Tsesarevich Nicholas Alexandrovich had no idea that he would inherit not only this ship, but the entire Russian Empire the following year. The new Emperor Nicholas II travelled to Copenhagen for the launching ceremony of the Imperial Yacht *Standart* on 21st March 1895.

In August 1907, Nicholas wrote to his mother, that " . . . he [Wilhelm II] so much liked the *Standart* that he said he would have been happy to get it as a present and that after such a yacht he was ashamed to show the *Hohenzollern*."

The Dowager Empress Maria Feodorovna replied: "I am sure the beautiful lines of the *Standart* would be an eyesore to Wilhelm. Still, his joke about how happy he would be if the yacht were given him as a present was in very doubtful taste. "

"I hope he will not have the cheek to order himself one here, this would really be the limit, though just like him, with the tact that distinguishes him!"[2]

Floating palace

On 8th September 1896, the *Standart* made its first voyage [without sea trials] to England. The British called the yacht a "floating palace". Black lacquered body, furniture made of fine wood, and embossed leather [instead of wallpaper], were used for its construction and interior decoration.

The state of the art Imperial Yacht had 3 masts, a displacement of 5480 tons, a length of 128 m, a width of 15.8 m, a draft of 6.6 m, a design speed of 22 knots, 24 boilers and 2 propellers.

Armament – eight 47-mm guns. The sharp clipper-head bow of the *Standart* was decorated with a

Views of the elegant and state of the art Imperial Yacht *Standart*

Pavel Dybenko and his common-law wife Alexandra Kollontai

gilded double-headed eagle. The crew numbered 373 officers and sailors, for whom the Emperor knew each one by name.

On the main deck (above the engine room) were the imperial cabins. Each block of cabins for the Emperor, Empress and Dowager Empress consisted of a living room, bedroom and bathroom. The same deck housed the dining room, the saloon, the cabins of the grand dukes and princesses, the yacht officers and the ship's wardroom.

On the lower deck there were cabins for children of the Imperial Family, rooms for servants, crew quarters and showers. The same deck housed a radio room, dynamo enclosures, workshops and some storerooms. Below this deck, in the bow of the yacht, there was a cargo hold and a powder magazine, and in the stern – refrigerators for perishable provisions. For the crew, much better living conditions have been created than on previous Imperial yachts.

What happened to Standart after the revolution?

In 1917, those very sailors, personally selected by Nicholas II, took part first in the February and then in the October Revolution. The central revolutionary organ of the Baltic sailors, Tsentrobalt[3], set up their headquarters in the former Emperor's study. Not only did they loot the ship's expensive wood and silk, they even took the Romanovs' family silver. "The chairman of Tsentrobalt Pavel Dybenko and his common-law wife Alexandra Kollontai slept in Nicholas II's bedroom. That is, they enjoyed all the benefits of the Imperial Yacht's previous owners, the very same ones the Bolsheviks condemned and accused of living better than the common Russian people", – writes Vladimir Shigin.

In the spring of 1918, the *Standart* took part in the Ice Campaign[4], following an order issued by Vladimir Lenin to save the Baltic Fleet from anti-Bolshevik forces.

In 1918, having lost its guards status and renamed March 18 (in memory of the first day of the Paris Commune), the yacht was mothballed and laid up for many years in the Military Harbour of Kronstadt.

Between 1933-36, the former imperial yacht was converted into a minelayer in Leningrad. By order of the commander of the Naval Forces of the Baltic Sea Lev Mikhailovich Haller (1883-1950) of 22nd January 1934, renamed *Marti*, after the French communist and secretary of the Comintern[5] – André Marty (1886-1956).

On 25th December 1936, the *Marti* officially be-came part of the KBF[6]. The ship was equipped with the latest devices for laying 320 mines, pow-erful artillery weapons (four 130-mm main guns, seven 76.2-mm universal guns, three 45-mm anti-aircraft guns and two coaxial machine guns). New steam engines were installed, providing a speed of over 14 knots and a cruising range of up to 2,300 miles.

In 1938, the ship became the flagship of the Baltic Fleet's barrage and trawling formation. In 1939, the ship laid mines off the coast of Finland, for which she received a commendation from the Mili-tary Council of the Baltic Fleet. In the summer of 1941, *Marti*'s crew won the Red Banner Challenge of the People's Commissariat of the Navy .

Naval battles with the participation of *Marti* during the Second World War

The *Marti* entered combat duty on 23rd June 1941. On 25th June, while performing a combat mission,

The *Standart* was renamed *Marti* after the French communist Andre Marty

A still from the Soviet film *"Мичман Панин"* ["Warrant Officer Panin"]. 1960

Marti sank an enemy submarine. In September of the same year, it repulsed a German air raid. The ship withstood bombardment of ten enemy bombers.

In early November 1941, the *Marti* took part in the evacuation of the defenders of the Hanko Peninsula. Despite the damage sustained by a mine explosion, *Marti* took on board and transported to Kronstadt 2,029 soldiers, 60 guns, 11 mortars, shells and food, and about 800 tons of cargo.

On 3rd April 1942, *Marti* was one of the first in the fleet to receive the honorary title of Guards Units [7]. The *Marti* was awarded the honour again in 1948.

In 1948, the very same French communist Andre Marty, whose name the ship bore, criticised both Stalin and the CPSU[8], in an article, published in the newspaper *L'Humanité*[9]. This was enough for the name of the Frenchman to be removed from all factories and ships, and a new name was chosen for the hero ship.

Traditionally, all mine layers in the Russian fleet, have been named after large Russian rivers or lakes. Thus *Marti* was renamed *Oka*, and was converted to a floating barracks. Under it's new name, the former Imperial Yacht served in the Soviet fleet until the end of the 1950s,

The film "Warrant Officer Panin"

The *Oka* embarked on its last voyage in the summer of 1960, when it was used as the auxiliary cruiser *Elizabeth* for the Soviet film *"Мичман Панин"* [Warrant Officer Panin] [10]. The film sounded the Imperial hymn *God Save the Tsar* one can only imagine the parallels? Thanks to the creators of the film, the ship can be seen in detail, including the engine room and the partially preserved interior decoration of the ship.

After filming, the ship was sent to its home harbor at Libau [today, Liepāja in Latvia] in the Baltic, where during exercises it served as a target for the testing of anti-ship missiles. In the mid-1960s, the former grand and luxurious Imperial Yacht was dismantled for scrap. Thus, one of the most famous Russian ships sunk into history.

NOTES:

[1] The frigate *Standart* was the first ship of Russia's Baltic fleet. Her keel was laid on 24th April 1703 at the Olonetsky shipyard near Olonets. She was the first flagship of the Imperial Russian Navy and was in service until 1727.

[2] Excerpted from *Dearest Mama . . . Darling Nicky: Letters Between Emperor Nicholas II and His Mother Empress Maria Feodorovna 1879-1917*, published privately in 2021.

[3] The Central Committee of the Baltic Fleet (Tsentrobalt) was a high-level elective revolutionary democratic body of naval enlisted men for coordination of the activities of sailors' committees of the Russian Baltic Fleet.

[4] The Ice Campaign was an operation which transferred the ships of the Baltic Fleet of the Imperial Russian Navy from their bases at Reval [Tallinn], and Helsinfors [Helsinki] to Kronstadt in 1918.

The Campaign was carried out in difficult ice conditions in February-May 1918. As a result of the operation, 236 ships and vessels were rescued from capture by German and Finnish troops and redeployed, including 6 battleships, 5 cruisers, 59 destroyers and 12 submarines.

[5] The Communist International (Comintern), was an international organization founded in 1919 that advocated world communism, controlled by the Soviet Union. The Comintern resolved to "struggle by all available means, including armed force, for the overthrow of the international bourgeoisie and the creation of an international Soviet republic as a transition stage to the complete abolition of the state"

[6] The Red Banner Baltic Fleet (KBF) was an operational-strategic formation of the Navy in the armed forces of the USSR during the Great Patriotic War (1941-45).

[7] Guards units were elite units and formations in the armed forces of the former Soviet Union. These units were awarded Guards status after distinguishing themselves in service, and are considered to have elite status. The Guards designation originated during the Great Patriotic War of 1941–45, its name coming from the Russian Imperial Guard, which was disbanded in 1917 following the Russian Revolution.

[8] The Communist Party of the Soviet Union.

[9] *L'Humanité* is a French daily newspaper. It was previously an organ of the French Communist Party.

[10] This Russian language film can be viewed on YouTube. Duration: 1 hour, 30 minutes

Zar Nikolaus und Kaiser Wilhelm während der Flottenmanöver

Nicholas II, Wilhelm II and the
1905 Treaty of Bjorkö

by Paul Gilbert

On 24th (O.S. 11th) July 1905 – Emperor Nicholas II and German Emperor Wilhelm II, met off the Finnish coast, where they signed the Treaty of Björkö, a secret Russian-German defense accord between the two empires. It was never ratified due to opposition from authoritative political circles on both sides, mainly because it was directed against existing alliance commitments between Russia and France.

On the evening of Sunday 23rd July 1905, the Kaiser arrived at Koivisto Sound from Viipuri Bay on his yacht, the Hohenzollern, dropping anchor near the Russian Imperial Yacht, the Polar Star.

Nicholas II transferred from the Polar Star in a launch, taking him to the SMS Berlin – which had escorted the German emperor's yacht – and lay anchor in the bay. He was greeted by Wilhelm II, who personally escorted his Russian cousin on an inspection tour of the newly commissioned cruiser of the German Imperial Navy.

Evidence of the meeting is given in telegrams that the two emperors exchanged, titled the Willy–Nicky correspondence. The letters were made public in 1917 by the new Provisional Government in Russia, and later translated to English.

Wilhelm II's efforts were linked to the Entente cordiale between France and England concluded in 1904 and at the same time tensions between England and Russia in the Russo-Japanese War of

1904-05, which raised hopes of drawing Russia to the side of the German Empire.

The Kaiser had been trying for some time to reach a treaty with Russia and on 27th October 1904 had a draft treaty sent to the Tsar, which he had worked out with Reich Chancellor von Bülow. In July 1905, due to political developments in Russia, the Kaiser finally saw an opportunity to realize it.

Wilhelm II was the chief author of the Treaty of Björkö, also known as the Treaty of Koivisto, but he acted without first consulting with his ministers. This secret mutual defence treaty was signed at a meeting that had been arranged by Wilhelm himself only four days beforehand.

The initiative to conclude a treaty belonged to German diplomacy, which sought to destroy the Russian-French alliance and prevent the creation of the Entente. To this end, it was supposed to turn the Russian-German alliance into a tripartite Russian-German-French, directed against Great Britain, the traditional rival of Russia (in Asia) and France (in Africa).

The overall defence treaty contained four articles and was signed by Emperors Wilhelm II and Nicholas II, and countersigned by Heinrich von Tschirschky (1858-1916), head of the German Foreign Office, and Aleksei Birilev (1844-1915), a member of the State Council of the Russian Empire and minister of the Russian Imperial Navy.

Treaty of Björkö

Their Majesties the Emperors of all the Russias and Germany, in order to ensure the continuance of peace in Europe have decreed the following Articles of a Defensive Alliance Treaty.

Article I

In case one of the two Empires is attacked by a European Power, his ally will help it in Europe with all its land and sea forces.

Article II

High Contracting Parties undertake not to conclude separate peace with any common adversary.

Article III

The present Treaty shall enter into force as soon as peace between Russia and Japan is concluded and shall remain valid as long as it is not denounced a year in advance.

Article IV

The Emperor of all the Russias, after the entry into force of this treaty, will take the necessary steps to initiate France to this agreement and engage it to join as an ally.

Reaction

The treaty needed to be ratified by both the German and Russian governments.

Germany

The driving motive for the treaty on the German side was to undermine the Franco-Russian Alliance and to strengthen Germany's position vis-à-vis Britain. Initially drafted as a global mutual defence pact, Wilhelm's insertion of the words "en Europe" into the first article, thereby restricting the treaty's remit to Europe, put the Kaiser at odds with the German Reich Chancellor, Bernhard von Bülow, who had not been forewarned of the late amendment. Bülow took the view that Russia's support would be needed in relation to the British presence in India, but Wilhelm thought such operations would just draw Germany into a fruitless war in that region at the expense of Germany's position

The Russian Imperial Yacht *Polar Star*

The German Imperial Yacht *Hohenzollern*

The cruiser *SMS Berlin* of the German Imperial Navy, escorted the German Imperial Yacht *Hohenzollern*

Emperor Nicholas II pulls up alongside the *SMS Berlin*

Emperors Nicholas II and Wilhelm II meet on the deck of the *SMS Berlin*

Emperors Nicholas II and Wilhelm II meet on the deck of the *SMS Berlin*

Emperor Nicholas II completes his review of the crew of the SMS Berlin

in Europe. Bülow threatened to resign over the disagreement, which prompted a melodramatic letter from the Kaiser ending with the words, "if a letter of resignation arrived from you, the next morning would find the Kaiser no longer alive! Think of my poor wife and children!" Bülow therefore offered to compromise, but before the issue could be resolved on the German side, the Russian government rejected the agreement.

Russia

Although Tsar Nicholas had signed the treaty, it was not ratified by his government because of the pre-existing Franco-Russian Alliance. Russian Prime Minister Sergei Witte and Foreign Minister Vladimir Lambsdorff had been neither present at the signing nor consulted beforehand; they insisted that the treaty should not come into effect unless it was approved and signed by France. Lambsdorff told the Tsar that it was "inadmissible to promise at the same time the same thing to two governments whose interests were mutually antagonistic". The Tsar gave in to their pressure, much to the consternation of the Kaiser, who reproached his cousin: "We joined hands and signed before God, who heard our vows!... What is signed, is signed! and God is our testator!" Wilhelm's chancellor, Count Bernhard von Bülow, however, also refused to sign the treaty because the Kaiser had added an amendment to the draft, against the advice of the Foreign Office, which limited the treaty to Europe

The initiative of Nicholas II met with resistance from the Russian government and the Foreign Ministry. V. N. Lamsdorf and S. Y. Witte managed to convince the emperor of the need to terminate the agreement. As a result, in November 1905, Nicholas II sent a letter to Wilhelm II, in which the effect of the Björko Treaty was conditional on the consent of France to join it. Formally, the Treaty of Björko was not terminated, but in fact it did not enter into force. At the same time, his actions frightened the French government and accelerated the provision of a large French loan.

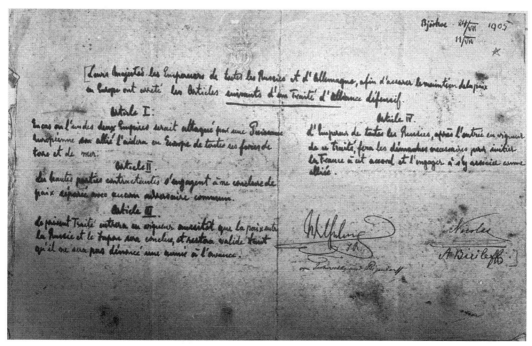

The Treaty of Björkö signed by Emperors Nicholas II and Wilhelm II on 24th (O.S. 11th) July 1905

Traitors or Heroes? Nicholas II's officers During the Great Patriotic War 1941-45

by Paul Gilbert

"Without the tsarist officers, the victory of the Reds in the Civil War would have been impossible"

– Leon Trotsky

Despite the Civil War and the repression of the 1930s, a significant number of former officers of the Russian Imperial Army and the Russian Army of the Provisional Government survived both the 1917 Revolution and the Civil War to serve under the Soviet regime during the Great Patriotic War (1941-45).

They played an important role as "military specialists" who trained the new generation of the Soviet military, transferring the traditions and spirit of the old Russian Imperial Army to the Red Army. Up to 40% of the entire officer corps of pre-revolutionary Russia joined the Bolsheviks and forge their victory. The head of the Revolutionary Military Council, Leon Trotsky (1879-1940), believed that without the tsarist officers, the victory of the Reds in the Civil War would have been impossible.

Tsarist officers contributed to the victory of the Soviet Union in the Great Patriotic War, by training of the armed forces and commanding the Red Army. Statistically – about 35% of all commanders of the Red Army divisions during the Great Patriotic War were officers of the old Imperial Army, 35% of the commanders at the fronts in 1941-1945, a third of the commanders and 13% of the comcors had become officers before 1917. Their presence in the infantry was especially great.

Many famous Soviet marshals and generals who impressed the world with their victories, were former officers of the Imperial Army. Among those were Georgy Konstantinovich Zhukov (1896-1974) who was awarded the St. George Cross twice for military merit, and promoted to the rank of non-commissioned officer for his bravery in battle. There were also men of higher rank, such as Apollon Yakovlevich Kruse (1892-1967), who served as Lieutenant General of the Red Army corps. The legendary Lieutenant General Dmitry Karbyshev (1880-1945), and Lieutenant General Alexander Bakhtin (1885-1963) had both sworn allegiance to Emperor Nicholas II.

But the most illustrious commanders of the Red Army in the war against Germany, consisted of five marshals of the USSR.

Alexander Mikhailovich Vasilevsky (1895-1977) had a strong Orthodox upbringing, his father was a priest, his mother was the daughter of a priest. He began his education in the local church school, and in 1909, he entered Kostroma seminary.

Vasilevsky began his military career during World War I, earning the rank of captain by 1917. Noted for his energy and personal courage, he took part in the famous Brusilov Offensive in 1916. After the October Revolution of 1917 and the start of the Civil War of 1917–1922 he was conscripted into the Red Army, taking part in the Polish-Soviet War of 1919–1921.

Vasilevsky served as a Russian career-officer in the Red Army, attained the rank of Marshal of the Soviet Union in 1943. He served as the Chief of the General Staff of the Soviet Armed Forces (1942-1945) and Deputy Minister of Defense during World War II, and as Minister of Defense from 1949 to 1953. As the Chief of the General Staff from 1942

to 1945, Vasilevsky became involved in planning and coordinating almost all the decisive Soviet offensives in World War II, from the Stalingrad counteroffensive of November 1942 to the assaults on East Prussia (January–April 1945), Königsberg (January–April 1945) and Manchuria (August 1945).

Fedor Ivanovich Tolbukhin (1894-1949) volunteered for the Imperial Army in 1914 at the outbreak of World War I. He was steadily promoted, and appointed to captain by 1916 under Emperor Nicholas II. He was also decorated for bravery multiple times.

In August 1918 Tolbukhin joined the Red Army, where he served as the chief of staff of the 56th infantry division. After the Russian Civil War ended (1921), Tolbukhin was given a number of staff positions.

Tolbukhin took part in the opening phases of Operation Barbarossa until August 1941, when he was made the chief of staff of the Crimean Front, which he held until March 1942. From May to July 1942, he was the assistant commander of the Stalingrad Military District. After that, he was the commander of the 58th Army until March 1943, and was involved in the Battle of Stalingrad, where Tolbukhin's superior, Colonel-General Andrei Yeremenko, praised his command organization and military prowess. On September 12, 1944, Tolbukhin was promoted to Marshal of the Soviet Union.

Tolbukhin is generally regarded as one of the finest Soviet generals of World War II. Meticulous, careful, and not overly ambitious like some Soviet commanders, Tolbukhin was well respected by fellow commanders and also his men, especially since he had a dedication to keeping casualty rates low. Tolbukhin was the recipient of numerous awards

Alexander Mikhailovich Vasilevsky (1895-1977)

and medals including the highest Soviet medal and rank, the Victory Order and Hero of the Soviet Union, respectively.

Colonel Boris Mikhailovich Shaposhnikov (1882-1945) joined the army of the Russian Empire in 1901 and graduated from the Nicholas General Staff Academy in 1910, reaching the rank of colonel in the Caucasus Grenadiers division in September 1917 during World War I. Also in 1917, he supported the Russian Revolution, an act unusual for an officer of his rank, and in May 1918 joined the Red Army.

Shaposhnikov was one of the few Red Army commanders with formal military training, and in 1921 he became 1st Deputy Chief of Staff of the Army's General Staff, where he served until 1925. He was appointed commander of the Leningrad Military District in 1925 and then of the Moscow Military District in 1927. From 1928 to 1931 he served as Chief of the Staff of the Red Army.

In May 1940 he was appointed a Marshal of the Soviet Union. Despite his background as a Tsarist officer, Shaposhnikov won the respect and trust of Stalin. His status as a professional officer—he did not join the Communist Party until 1939—may have helped him avoid Stalin's suspicions.

Fortunately for the Soviet Union, Shaposhnikov had a fine military mind and high administrative skills. He combined these talents with his position in Stalin's confidence to rebuild the Red Army leadership after the purges. He obtained the release from the Gulag of 4,000 officers deemed necessary for this operation. In 1939 Stalin accepted Shaposhnikov's plan for a rapid build-up of the Red Army's strength. Although the plan was not completed before the German invasion of June 1941, it had advanced sufficiently to save the Soviet Union

from complete disaster.

Leonid Aleksandrovich Govorov (1897-1955), was mobilized in December 1916, and sent to the Konstantinovskye Artillery School, from which he graduated in 1917. He became an artillery officer with the rank of podporuchik.

When the Russian Revolution broke out and the Russian Imperial Army disintegrated, Govorov returned home, but was conscripted into the White Guard army of Aleksandr Kolchak in October 1918, serving in an artillery battery in the Russian Civil War. Govorov fought in the Spring Offensive of the Russian Army, a general drive westwards by White forces in the east. He deserted in November 1919, fleeing to Tomsk, where he took part in an uprising against White authorities as part of a fighting squad. Govorov joined the Red Army in January 1920, serving in the 51st Rifle Division as an artillery battalion commander. With the division, he fought in the Siege of Perekop in November, during which Soviet forces drove Pyotr Wrangel's White Army out of Crimea.

In World War II, Govorov rose to command an army in November 1941 during the Battle of Moscow. He commanded the Leningrad Front from April 1942 to the end of the war. He reached the rank of Marshal of the Soviet Union in 1944, was awarded the title of Hero of the Soviet Union and many other awards.

Ivan Khristoforovich Baghramyan (1897-1982), joined the Russian Imperial Army as a volunteer on 16 September 1915. He was assigned as a private to the 116th Reserve Battalion and sent to Akhaltsikhe for basic training. With his training complete in December, he joined the 2nd Caucasus Frontier Regiment of the Russian Expeditionary Corps, which was sent to dislodge the Ottomans in

Fedor Ivanovich Tolbukhin (1894-1949)

Boris Mikhailovich Shaposhnikov (1882-1945)

Leonid Aleksandrovich Govorov (1897-1955)

Ivan Khristoforovich Baghramyan (1897-1982)

Persia. Bagramyan participated in several battles in Asadabad, Hamedan and Kermanshah, the Russian victories here sending Ottoman forces reeling toward Anatolia.

Learning about the exploits of the men in the outfit, the chief of staff of the regiment, General Pavel Melik-Shahnazaryan, advised Bagramyan to return to Tiflis to enroll in the Praporshchik Military Academy. But in order to attend the school, Bagramyan needed to satisfy the academy's requirement of having completed school at a gymnasium. This did not deter him and, after preparing for the courses in Armavir, he passed his exams and began attending the academy on February 13, 1917. He graduated in June 1917 and was assigned to the 3rd Armenian Infantry Regiment, stationed near Lake Urmia. But with the overthrow of the Russian Provisional Government in the midst of the October Revolution of 1917, his unit was demobilized.

Bagramyan's experience in military planning as a chief of staff allowed him to distinguish himself as a capable commander in the early stages of the Soviet counter-offensives against Nazi Germany. He was given his first command of a unit in 1942, and in November 1943 received his most prestigious command as the commander of the 1st Baltic Front. As commander of the Baltic Front, he participated in the offensives which pushed German forces out of the Baltic republics.

Bagramyan was a Soviet military commander and Marshal of the Soviet Union of Armenian origin. During World War II, Bagramyan was the second non-Slavic military officer, after Latvian Max Reyter, to become a commander of a Front. He was among several Armenians in the Soviet Army who held the highest proportion of high-ranking officers in the Soviet military during the war.

* * *

It seems ironic that "Nicholas the Bloody" should play a much greater role in the history of 20th century Russia, than the Soviets would ever give him credit for. It is thanks to the excellent training during the reign of Russia's last emperor, that former soldiers of the Russian Imperial Army should live through the 1917 Revolution and the Civil War to become marshals and generals, who fought heroic battles during the Great Patriotic War of 1941-45.

It is important to recognize that each of them committed treason by breaking their oath of allegiance to Emperor Nicholas II and the Russian Empire, but should they be condemned? Certainly not. These marshals and generals, demonstrated sincere patriotism and a willingness to sacrifice themselves for the Soviet Union, and saved the country from certain oblivion at the hands of the Nazi war machine. Their acts of bravery saved the lives of millions of Russians, had they not pushed the invaders back to Berlin, we may very well be living in a very different world today.

PAUL GILBERT © 2023

Lost architectural monuments of the Moscow Kremlin

by Paul Gilbert

During the Soviet years, numerous architectural monuments of the Moscow Kremlin were lost. Churches, monasteries, and palaces were destroyed because they reminded the Soviet regime under Stalin of Holy Russia and the glorious history of the Russian Empire.

The early 20th century postcard (above) reflects some of the greatest architectural losses in the Moscow Kremlin during the late 1920s to early 1930s – please refer to the numbers and the accompanying images below for additional information about each respective monument . .

1 – The Maly Nikolayevsky Palace or Small Nicholas Palace was a three-storey building located in the Kremlin on the corner of Ivanovskaya Square. Originally built in 1775, it served as the official Mos-

cow residence of Imperial Family up until the construction of the Grand Kremlin Palace in 1838-1849. The palace was a favourite residence of Grand Duke Nicholas Pavlovich (future Emperor Nicholas I). On 29th (O.S. 17th) April 1818, his son, the future Alexander II, was born in the palace, who considered it the home of his childhood. Between 1891 and 1905, the palace became a residence of Grand Duke Sergei Alexandrovich during his years as Governor-General of Moscow.

During the October armed uprising of 1917 in Moscow, the Small Nicholas Palace became the headquarters of the Junkers [a military rank in the Russian Guard and Army, until 1918] who were supporting the Committee of Public Security. The building became a target for the Red Guards and suffered more than other Kremlin buildings.

1 – The Maly Nikolayevsky Palace or Small Nicholas Palace; 2 and 2a – The first Monument to Emperor Alexander II; 3 – The Voznesensky (Ascension) Convent known as the Starodevichy Convent or Old Maidens' Convent; 4 – The two chapels at the Spassky Gates; 5 – The Church of Konstantin and Elena

NOTE: the photo at the top of the opposite page, shows the location of the above architecural monuments within the Kremlin.

According to Metropolitan Nestor (1885-1962): "The Small Nicholas Palace... suffered greatly from gunfire. Huge holes in the building's' façade are visible from the outside. Inside, too, everything is destroyed, and when I walked around the rooms, I saw a picture of complete destruction. Huge mirrors and other furnishings were barbarously broken and destroyed. The cabinets are broken, books, files and papers are scattered throughout the rooms... The palace church was hit by a shell and destroyed. The iconostasis was broken, the royal gates were forced open by explosions, and the veil of the church was torn in two. Hence, many valuable icons were stolen."

In 1929, the palace was demolished together with the adjacent Chudov and Ascension monasteries. In 1932-1934 the Kremlin Presidium (aka Building No. 14) was built on the site. It housed, first, the Supreme Soviet, i. e. the supreme legislative body of the Soviet Union until its dissolution in 1991, and, second, the offices of the Presidential Administration of Russia until 2011. The Kremlin Presidium was demolished in 2016.

2 – The first Monument to Emperor Alexander II stood above the Kremlin's Taynitsky Gardens facing the Moskva River. Work on the monuments was begun under Emperor Alexander III in 1893, and was completed five years later under Emperor Nicholas II in 1898.

The monument was the work of sculptor Alexander Opekushin (1838-1923), artist Peter Zhukovsky (1845-1912) and architect Nicholas V. Sultanov (1850-1908). The memorial consisted of a life-size bronze sculpture of Alexander II, set on a square pedestal with the words "To Emperor Alexander II by the love of the people" engraved on it. The sculpture was shaded by a canopy of polished dark red Karelian granite. The top of the canopy was made of specially fitted gilded bronze sheets with green enamel. On three sides, the monument was surrounded by a gallery with arches and open-work. Thirty-three mosaic portraits of Russia's rulers from Prince Vladimir to Emperor Nicholas II based on sketches by artist Peter Zhukovsky were placed in the gallery's vaults.

The solemn opening and consecration of the Monument to Emperor Alexander II took place on 16th August 1898. At eight in the morning, five cannon shots were fired from the Tainitskaya Tower. The opening ceremony began at two o'clock in the afternoon with a procession from the Chudov Monastery. After Metropolitan Vladimir of Moscow served a prayer service, the "Transfiguration March" was played and cannons were fired 360 times. The ceremony was closed by a parade of troops commanded by Emperor Nicholas II..

2a – The decree of the Council of People's Commissars of the Russian Soviet Federative Socialist Republic [supported by Lenin] dated 12th April 1918 called for all monuments of Russia's monarchs to be demolished and replaced with statues honouring the leaders of the revolution. The monument of Alexander II was to be one of the first monuments destroyed in this campaign. Lenin planned to install a monument to the writer Leo Tolstoy on the site, however, his plan never came to fruition.

The monument to Alexander II was demolished by the Bolsheviks in the summer of 1918. In June 1918, Russian art historian Nikolai Okunev described this event in his diary: "I saw in the cinema a newsreel on the removal of the monument to Alexander II in the Kremlin. It was terrible to watch! It's as if they were cutting a living person into pieces, and saying "Look, this is is how it's done!" It's not enough to show the shootings on the cinema screen." The

Small Nicholas Palace after the shelling of the Kremlin, 1917

The dismantled fragments of the Kremlin monument to Alexander II after its destruction in 1918. Situated between the two Tower is the Church of St. Catherine of the Ascension Monastery, blown up in 1929

remaining columns and gallery were demolished in 1928.

3 – The Voznesensky (Ascension) Convent known as the Starodevichy Convent or Old Maidens' Convent until 1817, was an Orthodox nunnery in the Moscow Kremlin which contained the tombs of grand princesses, tsarinas, and other noble ladies from the Muscovite royal court. The convent was founded at the beginning of the 15th century near the Kremlin's Spassky (Saviour's) Gate.

The convent was also used as a residence for royal fiancée's prior to their wedding. In 1721, the convent was renovated on behest of Peter the Great. In 1808, by order of Emperor Alexander I, the famous Italian architect Carlo Rossi (1775-1849) began construction of the Church of Saint Catherine, built in the Neo-Gothic design. During Napoleon's invasion of Moscow in 1812, the French army looted the monastery and expelled the nuns. Most of the property was preserved thanks to Abbess Athanasia, who managed to take the wealth from the sacristy to Vologda.

By 1907, the monastery had a mother superior, 62 nuns and 45 lay sisters. It was also in 1907, that the monastery celebrated the 500th anniversary of the death of the founder of the monastery St. Euphrosyne of Moscow (1353–1407). After the service, a procession took place, in which Grand Duchess Elizabeth Feodorovna participated, and placed a golden lamp and flower garlands on the founder's tomb.

During the October 1917 Revolution, the ancient buildings were damaged by artillery fire. In 1929, the convent complex – including the majestic 16th-century cathedral – was demolished by the Soviets in order to make room for the Red Commanders School, named after the All-Russian Central Executive Committee.

Some of the icons of Ascension Convent were transferred to the State Tretyakov Gallery and State museums of the Moscow Kremlin. The iconostasis of the Ascension Cathedral (see below) was moved into the Cathedral of Twelve Apostles (also in the Kremlin), while the tombs of the Muscovite royalty were transferred into an annex of the Archangel Cathedral, where they reside to this day.

4 – The two chapels at the Spassky Gates (facing Red Square) were built in the "Russian style" in 1866. Both belonged to St Basil's Cathedral. The left houses the sacred image of Our Lady of Smolensk as a reminder of the city's return to the Russian lands in the 16th century. The right is renowned for its sacred image of Christ the Saviour, an exact replica of the icon over Spassky Gates. They were both demolished in 1929.

The 16th-century icon was bricked over during the 1930s, and restored to its original in 2010.

5 – The Church of Konstantin and Elena in the lower section of the Kremlin Garden was built in 1692 by Tsarina Natalia Naryshkina, mother of Peter I. It was demolished in 1928. It became the first church demolished on the territory of the Kremlin since the Bolsheviks came to power and the first in a large series of losses of architectural monuments of the Moscow Kremlin in 1928-1930. Today the site is home to government buildings and a helipad for Russian president Vladimir Putin.

In addition, were the Chudov Monastery and the Monument to Grand Duke Sergei Alexandrovich:

6 – The Chudov Monastery (more formally known as Alexius' Archangel Michael Monastery) was

In 1930 the iconostasis of the Ascension Cathedral (below) was moved into the Cathedral of Twelve Apostles (also in the Kremlin), where it remains to this day

The Ascension Convent was destroyed in 1929

The Memorial Cross installed on the spot where Grand Duke Sergei Alexandrovich was assassinated

The Church of the Transfiguration of Christ the Saviour on Boru

founded in 1358 by Metropolitan Alexius of Moscow. The monastery was dedicated to the miracle of the Archangel Michael at Chonae on 19th September (O.S. 6th September). It was traditionally used for baptising the royal children, including future Tsars Feodor I, Aleksey I and Peter the Great.

The Chudov Monastery was demolished by the Bolsheviks in 1928, and the Presidium of the Supreme Soviet was built on the site. Grand Duke Sergei Alexandrovich's body was buried in a crypt of the Chudov Monastery. The burial crypt was located underneath a courtyard of that building, which was later used as a parking lot during the Soviet years. In 1990, building workers in the Kremlin discovered the blocked up entrance of the burial vault. The coffin was examined and found to contain the Grand Duke's remains, covered with the military greatcoat of the Kiev regiment, decorations, and an icon. He had left written instructions that he was to be buried in the Preobrazhensky Lifeguard regiment uniform, but as his body was so badly mutilated this proved impossible.

In 1995, the coffin was officially exhumed, and after a Panikhida in the Kremlin Cathedral of the Archangel, it was reburied in a vault of the Novospassky Monastery in Moscow on 17 September 1995.

7 – The Memorial Cross to Grand Duke Sergei Alexandrovich was consecrated on 2nd April 1908 on the spot where Grand Duke Sergei Alexandrovich was assassinated. The original bronze monument, set on a stepped pedestal of dark green labrador marble, was an example of 'Church Art Nouveau'. After the October 1917 Revolution, the cross was destroyed on 1st May 1918 by Bolshevik thugs with the personal participation of Vladimir Lenin.
On 4th May 2017, the memorial cross was restored in a ceremony that was attended by President Vladimir Putin and Patriarch Kirill of Moscow.

8 – The Church of the Transfiguration of Christ the Saviour on Boru was located in the courtyard of the Grand Kremlin Palace [seen in behind the church in the photo above]. The name "on Boru" came from the coniferous forests which once surrounded the church, that once stood on Borovitsky Hill.

In 1767, when Catherine II began the reconstruction of the Kremlin, the church was revived in brick and required major repairs.

The Church of the Savior-on-Boru was demolished on 1st May 1933 by order of the Politburo of the Central Committee of the CPSU, despite the protests of prominent restorers. The church's ancient bells were transferred to the funds of the Moscow Kremlin Museums. Upon demolition of the church, a 5-storey service building was built on the site of the cathedral. Plans to restore one of the oldest churches in Moscow have not yet been considered.

In 2014 President Vladimir Putin proposed the restoration of the former Chudov Monastery, Ascension Convent, and Small Nicholas Palace. Opposition from UNESCO ended any hope of reconstructing these architectural gems. The proposal, had it been approved, would have restored the historical vista of Ivanovskaya Square. Instead, it has become park space for tourists visiting the Kremlin museums and churches.

Nicholas II attends opening of a sanatorium in Alupka, 1913

by Paul Gilbert

In 1913 – the year marking the 300th anniversary of the Romanov Dynasty – Emperor Nicholas II and his family arrived in Crimea for a 4-month stay. From 14th August to 17th December, the Imperial family lived at the beautiful Livadia Palace, situated on the southern coast overlooking the Black Sea.

At the end of September 1913, a sanatorium named after Emperor Alexander III (1845-1894) was opened in Alupka for students and teachers of theological schools in Russia. It was an elongated three-story building, where on the east side the

premises of the third floor were intended for the church. The interior of the church was illuminated by a large bronze chandelier, and featured a marble iconostasis and solea[1].

This sanatorium was located in the western part of Alupka on land that once belonged to the Vorontsovs, whose heirs at the beginning of the 20th century divided it into plots for long-term lease. Plot No. 72 was rented free of charge by the Synod for a climatic sanatorium for teachers of parochial schools. In 1913, here, according to the project of the architect Nikolai Pavlovich Kozlov (1870-1926), at the expense of the School Council of Russia, a sanatorium building was erected, designed for 100 guests. The sanatorium had separate rooms, a well-equipped kitchen, a common refectory, and, most importantly, its own five-domed Church of St. Alexander Nevsky.

The church was consecrated in memory of the Emperor and his heavenly patron Saint Alexander Nevsky. The grand opening of the sanatorium in Alupka was attended by Emperor Nicholas II, his daughter Grand Duchess Maria Nikolaevna, Minister of the Imperial Court Count Vladimir Frederiks, local dignitaries and members of the clergy.

Here is an excerpt from the diary of Nicholas II for 22nd September 1913: "At 9 ½ I went with Maria and Frederiks to Alupka for the consecration of the Church of the Climatic Sanatorium for students of church schools. A beautifully arranged big house for 80 and even up to 100 guests."

Nicholas II accompanied by Grand Duchess Maria Nikolaevna, and his retinue arrived in front of the main entrance, which was decorated with garlands of flowers and canvases with imperial monograms. They were solemnly greeted by representatives of the city authorities, their wives and the clergy, headed by V.K. Sabler, who in 1911-1915 served as chief prosecutor of the Synod.

To perpetuate the historical event of Nicholas II's attendance at the consecration, court photographer K.F. Hahn and Alupka photographer A.E. Zimmerman, captured the historic event on camera.

Several photographs have survived to this day which show a general view of the sanatorium and the Church of St. Alexander Nevsky, the interior of the church and the arrival and procession headed by Emperor Nicholas II.

After the advent of Soviet power, by order of the Chief Commissioner for Crimea, the sanatorium for clergy, along with the church, among other noble estates of Alupka, were nationalized and became the property of the Russian People's Republic. In June 1923, the Presidium of the Executive Committee of the Crimea issued a decision to close the Alexander Nevsky Church and transfer the movable property of the temple to the Special Storage of the Yalta District Executive Committee. The liquidated church was transferred to the property of the administration of the sanatorium of the People's Commissariat of Railways (NKPS). In Soviet times, a climatic sanatorium named after V.I. F.E. Dzerzhinsky.

The Church of St. Alexander Nevsky suffered neglect and disrepair, and in 1927, the building sustained significant damage during an earthquake.

In the spring of 1996, through the efforts of the Crimean and Simferopol Metropolitan Lazarus, the building was returned to the Church, and now a sanitarium named after St. Luke of Crimea is located here. The Church of Alexander Nevsky was also restored, in which divine services are held, as well as a Sunday school.

Today, the five onion-shaped domes of St. Alexander Nevsky Church are visible from different vantage points in Alupka.

NOTES:

[1] a platform or a raised part of the floor in front of the inner sanctuary in an Eastern Orthodox church on which the singers stand and the faithful receive communion.

Nicholas II visiting the Emperor Alexander III Sanatorium in Alupka, 22nd September 1913

Nicholas II visiting the Emperor Alexander III Sanatorium in Alupka, 22nd September 1913

Nicholas II and the Boy Scout Movement in Russia

by Paul Gilbert

After reading the English language edition of Robert Baden-Powell's book *Scouting for Boys*, Nicholas II immediately issued an order for the translation and publication. An initial printing of 25,000 copies of the Russian edition of '*Юный Разведчик*' (Young Scout) were issued in 1908.

The book inspired a young Russian officer, Colonel Oleg Ivanovich Pantyukhov (1882-1973), to set up the first Russian Scout patrol the following year.

Colonel Oleg Ivanovich Pantyukhov was born in Kiev on 25 March 1882, to a family of a military physician and an anthropologist. From 1892 to 1899 he studied at Tifflis cadet school. During his studies he became a member of the group named Pushkin Club. The group was somehow similar to the modern Boy Scouts. Every weekend they went on hiking trips with camping in the nearby mountains.

From 1899 to 1901, Pantyukhov studied at the Pavlovsk Military School. After graduation he became an officer of the Leib Guard (Russian Imperial Guard) 1st infantry battalion stationed in Tsarskoye Selo. In 1908 he married Nina Mikhaylovna Dobrovolskaya, who later became one of the pioneers of the Girl Guide movement in Russia.

In 1908–09 Pantyukhov became acquainted with the works of Robert Baden-Powell and decided to

Robert Baden-Powell (1857-1941),

Colonel Oleg Ivanovich Pantyukhov (1882-1973)

try these ideas on Russian soil. He organized the first Russian Scout troop Бобр (Beaver) in Pavlovsk, on 30 April [O.S. 17 April] 1909. By late 1910 scout organizations existed in Tsarskoye Selo, St. Petersburg and Moscow.

Nicholas II extended a personal invitation to Baden-Powell to visit St. Petersburg and Moscow in December 1910 – January 1911. The Tsar personally received the Boy Scout leader in his study in the Alexander Palace on 2 January 1911.

"There was no ceremony about him," Baden-Powell recorded in his diary. "He shook hands and, speaking in very good English, asked me about my visit and then went on to talk about the Boy Scouts." They then had "a very cheery talk (no one else present) of over half an hour," after which they parted.

The Tsar had explained to Baden-Powell how he had ordered the translation and publication of the Boy Scout handbook and reviewed the first Russian Scout detachment, and went on to outline his hopes for the movement. According to Baden-Powell, Nicholas II was "much impressed by the possibilities which lay in the Movement for developing discipline, patriotism and character," he approved "teaching the boys by methods which really appealed to their imagination and keenness."

Baden-Powell departed fully convinced that the Tsar was absolutely sincere, and that he had "grasped the idea" of scouting. There is no question of Nicholas II's interest in scouting was clearly genuine. Apart from ordering the Russian publication of *Scouting for Boys*, he seems personally to have arranged to meet its author. With Baden-Powell installed in the Imperial capital's elegant

A copy of the second edition of *Юный Разведчик* (Young Scout), published in 1910. Priced at 1 ruble, 25 kopecks

A page from *Юный Разведчик* (Young Scout),
published in 1910. Priced at 1 ruble, 25 kopecks

Pantyukhov with scouts in 1915

Hotel de France, the Tsar could have left any official interview to one of his ministers. Instead, he issued a private invitation through the British Embassy, a request that apparently took his visitor by complete surprise. This encounter was also quite unlike those with his Ministers and Duma politicians, meetings that the Tsar could not avoid, however much he disliked the advice they forced upon him. Put differently, with Baden-Powell it was Nicholas and Nicholas alone who both took the initiative and the agenda, and had no need to disguise his opinions or dissemble behind a mask of good manners.

On 19 December 1910, Pantyukhov met in St. Petersburg with Baden-Powell, the pair becoming good friends. The latter invited Pantyukhov to visit Scout organizations in England, the Netherlands, Sweden and Denmark. On his return in 1912, he wrote the first Russian Scouting books *"Памятка Юного Разведчика"* (Handbook for the Young Scout) and *"В гостях у Бой-скаутов"* (Visiting the Boy Scouts). In 1913 he wrote *"Спутник Бойскаута"* (The Boy Scout Companion). Pantyukhov met Nicholas II and gifted him a Scouting badge for Tsesarevich Alexei, who formally became a Scout.

The first "scout bonfire" was lit on 30 April 1909 in Pavlovsk Park. After that, the Boy Scout movement spread rapidly across Russia and into Siberia. By 1917, there were 50,000 Scouts in 143 cities.

Emperor Nicholas II wholeheartedly supported the Scout movement ranks. The patron saint of the Russian scouts was the Holy Great Martyr George the Victorious.

During World War I Pantyukhov received the Cross of St. George, for bravery. During the October Revolution of 1917, he was the leader of the cadets who unsuccessfully defended the Kremlin from the Bolsheviks. In 1919 in Novocherkassk (controlled at the time by the White Army), Pantyukhov was unanimously elected the Chief Scout of Russia

With the advent of communism after the October Revolution of 1917, and during the Russian Civil War from 1917 to 1922, most of the Scoutmasters and many Scouts fought in the ranks of the White Army and interventionists against the Red Army. In 1918, a purge of the Scout leaders took place, in which many of whom perished under the Bolsheviks. Those Scouts who did not wish to accept the new Soviet system either left Russia for good, like Pantyukhov and others, or went underground.

However, clandestine Scouting did not last long. On 19 May 1922, all of those newly created organizations were united into the Young Pioneer organization of the Soviet Union (it existed until 1990). Since that year, Scouting in the Soviet Union was banned.

In closing, it is interesting to note that the quiet support of Nicholas II played a crucial role in the survival of the scouting movement in pre-revolutionary Russia. This fact is notable, since it is indicative of preferences and insights not usually associated with the last Tsar. If Baden-Powell is only partially correct in his assessment of Nicholas's motives, intentions, and a vision of a future Russia, the picture presented still suggests a man somewhat different from the shallow autocrat of legend.

Pantyukhov with scouts in 1915Tsarskoye Selo Boy Scout troop

The Imperial Railway Pavilion [aka as the The Tsar's Train Station] at Tsarskoye Selo and it's architect Vladimir Aleksandrovich Pokrovsky (1871-1931)

Update on the restoration of the Imperial Railway Pavilion at Tsarskoye Selo

by Paul Gilbert

Further to my announcement in *Sovereign* No. 12 Winter 2024[1], that the Imperial Railway Pavilion at Tsarskoye Selo[2] would be restored, I am pleased to provide the following update, which includes photos [taken in March 2024] of the progress being made on this important historic project, one which is closely connected to Emperor Nicholas II.

The building is currently hidden under scaffolding and outdoor construction hoarding, as experts carry out the restoration of the facade, it's historic elements and install a new roof. This work can be seen in the photos published in this article, all of which were taken in the spring.

The Imperial Railway Pavilion [aka as the Tsar's Train Station] is a registered cultural heritage site of federal significance, an act which saved the building from destruction. Despite the fact that the building has not been used since the 1930s, it has been preserved in fairly good condition. The unique building will be restored to its original. In addition to the building itself, the 200-meter passenger platform and canopy will be reconstructed and the unique paintings which once decorated the walls and ceilings of the interior, and which have been partially revealed by restorers, will be revived.

The next stage, after a detailed study, will be the design, and then the restoration. The concept of using the building as a museum after the completion of the work will also be worked out.

The restoration work on the Imperial Railway Pavilion is part of a comprehensive development proect which includes the nearby Feodorovsky Gorodok,

and other buildings to their original pre-revolutionary look.

The original wooden Imperial Railway Pavilion and the covered platform were constructed in 1895. They were intended to receive Imperial Trains arriving at Tsarskoye Selo through the Aleksandrovskaya Station, which is situated north of the pavilion on the St. Petersburg-Warsaw railway line.

On 25th January 1911, the wooden station was destroyed by fire. It was decided to erect a new stone building on the same site by the architect Vladimir Aleksandrovich Pokrovsky (1871-1931) with the participation of a graduate of the Academy of Arts Mikhail Ivanovich Kurilko (1880-1969).

The new pavilion was designed in the Neo-Russian Style beloved by Nicholas II. The Fepdorovsky Gorodok, the Feodorovsky Sovereign Cathedral, the Sovereign's Martial Chamber, and the barracks of His Majesty's Own Convoy were all built in the same style. Together, they form an architectural ensemble in which motifs of ancient Russian architecture were used. In addition, the planning and design of the Imperial Railwat Pavilion was influenced by the Imperial Railway Station, which has survived to this day at the Vitebsky Railway Station in St. Petersburg.

The front part of the building consists of three halls. In the center there is a square lobby with a front porch, large enough to accomodate automobiles and carriages. The halls on the sides of the vestibule were intended for the Emperor and his retinue: on the south side was the Tsar's Hall, on the north side – the Retinue Hall. A metal canopy was built above the platform and tracks, adjacent to the eastern façade of the station.

Paintings became an unusual decoration of the walls and ceilings of the building's interior. They were made using a tempera-glue technique on plaster. A unique painting has been partially preserved [see photo below] to this day, which will allow experts to restore it in full to its original.

During the First World War of 1914-1917, the Imperial Railway Pavilion was used to receive wounded Russian soldiers, who were transferred to the hospital established by the Empress Alexandra Feodorovna in the Feodorovsky Gorodok. And after the Revolution of 1917, it was renamed the Uritsky Pavilion and was used as a dormitory for workers of the Track Repair of the Mechanical Plant.

The Tsarist emblems were removed from the building's facade, and the ceremonial halls were divided by walls. The building began to lose its former grandeur and ceremonial appearance: the porch was adapted for the kitchen, furniture, lamps, objects of decorative and applied art were lost.

Now in the 21st century, a new life awaits the former Imperial Railway Pavilion. Following completion of the reconstruction of the building and restoration of the interiors, the Board of Trustees of the Tsarskoye Selo Station Foundation, will discuss proposals for the future use of the building.

NOTES:

[1] *'Imperial Railway Pavilion at Tsarskoye Selo is being restored'*, *Sovereign* No. 12 Winter 2024, pg. 49-56

[2] The Imperial Railway station at Tsarskoye Selo served as the main terminus for the two Imperial Trains of Emperor Nicholas II

Two views of the Imperial Railway Pavilion, covered in construction hoarding. March 2024

Scaffolding surrounds the Imperial Railway Pavilion, covered in construction hoarding. March 2024

Cleaning the interior have revealed the original colourful paintings on the walls and ceilings

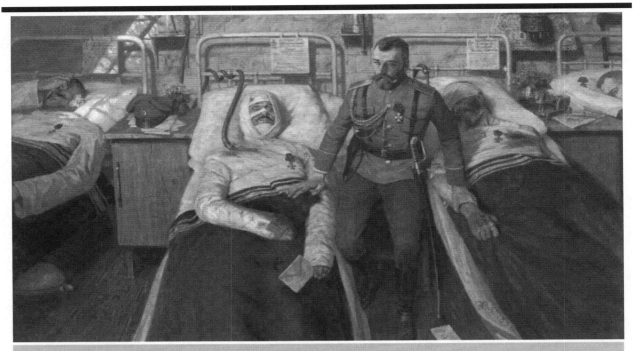

Healthcare reform under Nicholas II

by Paul Gilbert

During the 1920s, the Bolsheviks boasted of how they had improved healthcare in Russia after the overthrow of Nicholas II, however, this is just one more lie which the new order utilized in their campaign to discredit the reforms of Russia's last Tsar. And to this day, Nicholas II's detractors continue to claim that the Russian people "suffered" and that the Tsar did "nothing" to help them.

During the reign of Nicholas II, the population of the Russian Empire increased from 122 million in 1894 to 182 million in 1914 – an increase of 62 million! Given such a staggering increase in the country's population, Nicholas II's health care reforms were nothing short of impressive.

After Nicholas II ascended the throne in 1894, healthcare reform in the Russian Empire became the subject of special concern for the new Emperor. It was during his reign that the development of medicine and healthcare accelerated throughout the Russian Empire.

On 11th January 1897, Nicholas II approved a Special Commission on measures to prevent and combat plague, chaired by Duke Alexander Petrovich Oldenburg [1] whom the Tsar allowed to use the premises of the Emperor Alexander I Fort at Kronstadt for experimental anti-plague purposes. In October 1897, Oldenburg traveled to Turkestan to take emergency measures to prevent the plague from entering the Empire, for which he received "His Imperial Majesty's deepest gratitude for the labours incurred" for his efforts to spare European Russia and the rest of Europe from plague penetrating their borders.

Duke Alexander Petrovich of Oldenburg (1844-1932)

One of the main reasons for the spread of disease, was of course poor sanitation. As a result, in August 1908, Nicholas II advised the Minister of Internal Affairs to pay "serious attention to the dismal state of sanitation in Russia. It is necessary at all costs to achieve its improvement". The Emperor empha-sized the need to be able to "prevent epidemics, not just fight them". He demanded that the case of streamlining the sanitary-medical organization in Russia be urgently developed and submitted for legislative consideration.

Preparation of anti-bacterial plague drugs in the Plague Control Laboratory
of the Emperor Alexander I Fort at Kronstadt

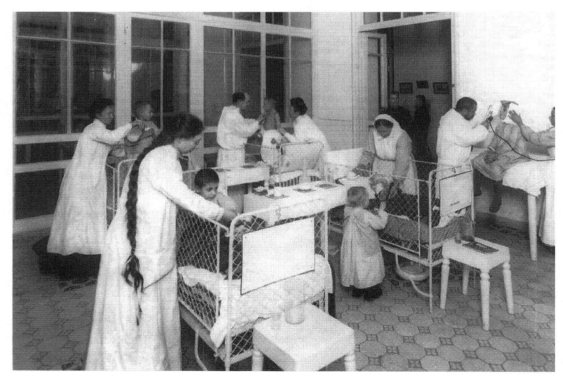

Medical examination of children in a children's clinic, St. Petersburg. 1903

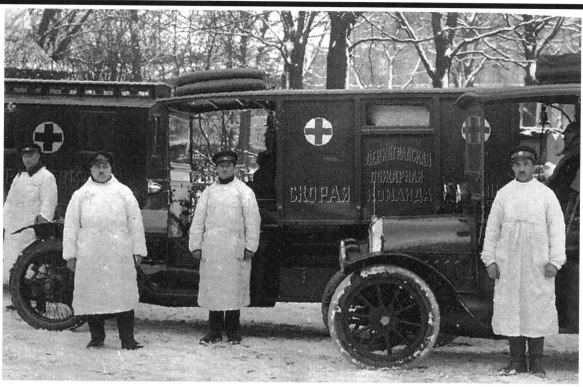

Russia's first ambulance station opened in St. Petersburg in 1899

In 1897, the Women's Medical Institute (the first medical institute of this kind in Russia)
opened in St. Petersburg

Various commissions were established during Nicholas II's reign to prevent the occurrence of highly infectious diseases. In March 1912, the Emperor approved the Interdepartmental Commission for the revision of medical and sanitary legislation, writing in the margins of the Journal of the Council of Ministers: "This is to be done at an accelerated pace." The head of the commission was appointed the chairman of the Medical Council of the Ministry of Internal Affairs, honorary life surgeon academician Georgy Ermolaevich Rein (1854-1942). In the spring of 1912, the commission presented its project for the transformation of the central and local authorities of medical and sanitary affairs. After reviewing it, Nicholas II noted: "Submit to the Council of Ministers. Continue to conduct business at an accelerated rate. "

Nicholas II supported the introduction of a territorial system of medical districts within the Russian Empire, a system not found anywhere else in the world at the time. This system was later adopted by the Bolsheviks, who appropriated its authorship. In the course of the health care reform in the Russian Empire, a three-tier structure of medical assistance to the population was formed: a medical department, a county hospital, and a provincial hospital. Treatment in these health facilities was free of charge.

The opening of new hospitals and medical institutions developed at a rapid pace. The number of hospitals increased from 2,100 in 1890 to 8,110 in 1912 and 8,461 in 1916 +170 psychiatric hospitals. The number of hospital beds increased from 70,614 in 1890 to 227,868 in 1916. The number of doctors also increased from 13,000 in 1890 to 22,772 doctors in 1914 and 29,000 in 1916.

In addition, there were 5,306 medical districts and paramedic points. By 1914 there were 28,500 medical assistants, 14,194 midwives, 4,113 dentists, 13,357 pharmacies. In 1913, 8,600 students studied at 17 medical universities.

In 1901, 49 million people received medical care in Russia, three years later, in 1904 – 57 million, in 1907 – 69 million, in 1910 – 86 million and in 1913 – 98 million. These efforts led to a significant decrease in overall mortality. In the period 1906-1911 there were 29.4 deaths per thousand inhabitants, 26 deaths per thousand in 1911, and 25 per thousand in 1912.

Mortality from smallpox decreased 2.5 times, from typhus decreased 2 times, from acute childhood diseases decreased 1.4 times. In the period from 1891 to 1895 – 587 thousand people died on average from acute infectious diseases, and steadily decreased during the period from 1911 to 1914 to 372 thousand people.

On 19th March 1899, Russia's first ambulance station was opened in St. Petersburg.

Under Nicholas II, Russian scientific medicine received world recognition, which could not have developed without state support. For the first time, Russian medical scientists were awarded the Nobel Prize: physiologist Ivan Petrovich Pavlov (1904) and microbiologist Ilya Ilyich Mechnikov (1908). Russian medical science carried out pioneering studies of the structure of the brain, and the origins of such fields of medicine as forensic psychiatry, gynecology and hygiene. At the beginning of the 20th century. more than 150 general and specialized scientific medical journals were published in Russia.

Despite the advancements in health care in the Russian Empire, serious health problems remained. For instance, at the beginning of the 20th century Russia experienced a high mortality rate from common widespread infections: plague, smallpox, cholera, typhoid. It was not until the 1940s and the invention of antibiotics did things improve.

Infant mortality under Nicholas II steadily declined. The downward trend in mortality (both children and adults) began before the revolution. According to statistics, the death rate during the reign of Nicholas II per 1000 people had been steadily decreasing.

Emperor Nicholas II also made efforts to fight against drunkenness. Both the Tsar and Russian society, considered the situation with drunkenness in Russia depressing. Russian historian and journalist Sergei Sergeiivich Oldenburg (1888-1940) wrote that in 1913, "The Tsar, during his trip to the Russian provinces, saw bright manifestations of gifted creativity and labour; but next to this, with deep sorrow, one saw sad pictures of national weakness, family poverty and abandoned households – the inevitable consequences of a drunken life."

In 1913, the year marking the 300th anniversary of the House of Romanov, Emperor Nicholas II stated that he "came to the firm conviction that the welfare of the treasury should not be made dependent on the ruin of my loyal subjects."

From 1914, schools of the Ministry of Public Education have been instructed to teach high school students a course in hygiene with the obligatory reporting of information about the dangers of alcohol. In March 1914, the Holy Synod of the Russian Orthodox Church decided to establish a national day of sobriety on 29th August[2], the day of the Beheading of John the Baptist. This holiday was held annually and collected donations for the fight against drunkenness.

By 1913, there were about 1,800 temperance societies in Russia with a total number of members of more than half a million.

As a result of this important decision of Nicholas II, serious changes took place in the country, affecting both the private life of people and their health, and the economy of Russia. The Emperor noted: "Sobriety is the basis of the well-being of the people."

On 11th August 1908, Emperor Nicholas II initiated the creation of a unified state health care system. In July 1914, a few days before the outbreak of World War I, a bill to create the Ministry of Health was introduced to the Council of Ministers. On 1st September 1916, the Chairman of the Medical Council of the Russian Empire, Honorary Life Surgeon, Academician Georgy Ermolaevich Rein (1854-1942), who held these duties until 27th February 1917. Thus, Georgy Ermolaevich became the first and last Minister of Health of the Russian Empire.

NOTES:

[1] Duke Alexander Petrovich of Oldenburg was a Russian Infantry General, adjutant-general, senator and member of the State Council of the Russian Empire. He was the father-in-law of Nicholas II's younger sister Grand Duchess Olga Alexandrovna (1882-1960), who was married to his only son Duke Peter Alexandrovich (1868-1924), from August 1901 to October 1916.

[2] A national Day of Sobriety was revived in 21st century Russia, today an unofficial Russian holiday instituted by the Russian Orthodox Church. The date of 11th September (O.S. 29th August) was chosen because on this day Orthodox Christians celebrate the Beheading of the Holy and Glorious Prophet, Forerunner and Baptist John. On this day, the faithful are expected to observe a strict fast, which includes abstinence from alcohol.

"Judge not, lest ye be judged" —
In defence of the last Russian Empress

by Paul Gilbert

In a letter to his mother dated 8th June 1910, Nicholas II expresses his deep concern and anxiety about his wife's condition . . .

"I am completely run down mentally by worrying over her health."

Over the past 5 years, I have posted many photos of Empress Alexandra Feodorovna on my personal Facebook page, but I am sadly disheartened by the numerous bitter, nasty comments often left by people. This poor woman has been criticized for everything from "never smiling", "looking miser-

able" or depicting a "sour face" – just to name a few.

Just last week I received a nasty email from a Facebook troll who noted how much Alexandra is "hated" by "noted historians".

During her life, Alexandra carried much grief, worry and sorrow on her shoulders, all of which began at an early age. She lost her brother Friedrich to haemophilia in May 1873; her sister Marie died of diphtheria in November 1878; and the following month, her beloved mother Princess Alice also died of diphtheria in December 1878.

After her mother and sister's deaths, Alix became more reserved and withdrawn. She described her childhood before her mother and sister's death as "unclouded, happy babyhood, of perpetual sunshine, then of a great cloud."

In March 1892, her father Grand Duke Louis IV, died of a heart attack. According to Baroness Sophie Buxhoeveden, Alix regarded the death of her father as perhaps "the greatest sorrow of her life". Buxhoeveden recalled in her 1928 biography [The Life and Tragedy of Alexandra Feodorovna] that "for years she could not speak of him, and long after when she was in Russia, anything that reminded her of him would bring her to the verge of tears". This loss was probably so much greater for Alix because Grand Duke Louis IV had been Alix's only remaining parent since she was six years of age.

Alexandra's health was never robust and her five pregnancies, wreaked havoc on her body. Some historians attribute the semi-invalidism of her later years to nervous exhaustion from obsessive worry over the fragile health of her son. She spent most of her time in bed or reclining on a chaise in her boudoir or on a veranda. This immobility enabled her to avoid the social occasions that she found distasteful. Alexandra regularly took a herbal medicine known as Adonis Vernalis in order to regulate her pulse. She was constantly tired, slept badly, and complained of swollen feet. She ate little, but never lost weight – she had become a vegetarian. She may have suffered from Graves Disease (hyperthyroidism), a condition resulting in high levels of the thyroid hormone, which can also result in atrial fibrillation, poor heartbeat and lack of energy.

After the birth of Alexei, the long awaited heir to the Russian throne, Alexandra felt guilt for having passed haemophilia to her son. Most historians believe that she had a breakdown due to the constant worry for her son's health, and later perhaps suffered from mental health issues.

From the day which she arrived in St. Petersburg, members of the Imperial Family, along with the ladies of the aristocracy took a particular dislike to Russia's new Empress. Alexandra was a deeply religious woman, and she took great lengths to keep both herself and later he children at a distance from the debauchery of the capital.

Alexandra was also isolated for being foreign. Increasingly, she became an even more unpopular figure with the Imperial Family, the aristocracy, and the Russian people for numerous reasons, including her association with Rasputin and Anna Vyrubova. During the Great War, she became unpopular because of her German birth and upbringing, when that country was an enemy of the Russian Empire. Alexandra became a primary focus for the increasing unrest associated with opposition to the monarchy.

Whatever her shortcomings as Empress, let us be more careful in the words we choose before we pass judgement on this poor woman.

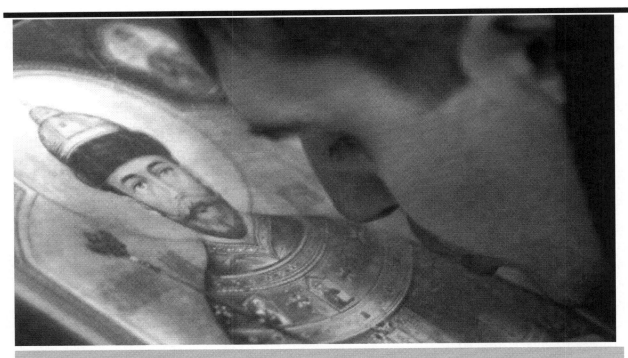

The Veneration of Tsar-Martyr Nicholas II

by Paul Gilbert

The veneration of Nicholas II, his wife Alexandra Feodorovna and their five children, who were murdered by members of the Ural Soviet [Bolsheviks] in Ekaterinburg on the night of 16/17 July 1918, by Orthodox believers, actually began shortly after their deaths. The most significant result of the veneration was the canonization of Nicholas II and his family as martyrs in 1981 by the Russian Orthodox Church Outside of Russia (ROCOR) and as passion-bearers by the Russian Orthodox Church of the Moscow Patriarchate in 2000.

Veneration of the Tsar's Family is expressed in iconography, veneration of relics, dedication of churches, memorial crosses, installation of monuments, and various ceremonies. Cross processions dedicated to the Tsar's Family are held in Russia, attract more and more faithful each year. Ekaterin-burg has become the center of veneration of the Tsar's Family. The Ural capital has done more to honour Nicholas II and his family than any other city in Russia.

Once a bastion of Bolshevism, Ekaterinburg has slowly shed its status as the "capital of atheism". Since the fall of the Soviet Union in 1991, the Urals has experienced a revival of faith, with Ekaterinburg as the center of Orthodoxy in the region.

"Silent" veneration

Almost immediately after the announcement of the execution of Nicholas II and his family, sentiments began to emerge in certain groups of believers in Russian society, which decades later led to their canonization.

Three days after the shooting, on 21st July (O.S. 8th) 1918, during a Divine Liturgy in the Kazan Cathedral in Moscow, Patriarch Tikhon delivered a sermon in which he outlined the "essence of the spiritual feat" of the Tsar and the attitude of the church to the question of execution: "A terrible thing happened the other day: the former Tsar Nicholas Alexandrovich was shot... We must, in obedience to the teaching of the word of God, condemn this deed, otherwise the blood of the Tsar will fall on us, and not only on those who committed it. We know that when he abdicated the throne, he did so for the good of Russia and out of love for it. He could have found security and a comparatively quiet life abroad after his abdication, but he did not do so, wanting to suffer with Russia. He did nothing to improve his situation, he resigned himself to his fate without complaint." In addition, Patriarch Tikhon blessed the archpastors and pastors to perform *pannikhidas* [memorial service for the dead] for the Imperial Family.

In the opinion of the Russian Orthodox Church, the reverent respect for the anointed one, the tragic circumstances of his death at the hands of his enemies, and the pity aroused by the death of innocent children – all this gradually formed an attitude towards the Imperial Family not as victims of political struggle, but as Christian martyrs. As Metropolitan Yuvenaly of Krutitsy and Kolomna noted, "the veneration of the Tsar's Family, begun by Tikhon, continued, despite the prevailing ideology, throughout several decades of the Soviet period of our history. Clergy and laity lifted up prayers to God for the repose of the murdered victims, members of the Imperial Family. In people's houses in towns and villages photographs of the Tsar and his family were displayed." Unfortunately, there is no record on the extent of this veneration.

In the *émigré milieu*, these sentiments were even

more evident. For example, in 1947 there were reports in the émigré press about miracles performed by the Royal Martyrs. In a 1991 interview, Metropolitan Anthony of Sourozh, describing the situation among Russian émigrés, pointed out that "many abroad venerate them as saints. Those who belong to the Patriarchal Church or other churches perform *pannikhidas* in their memory, or even *molebens* [a liturgical service of supplication or thanksgiving]. And privately, they consider themselves free to pray to them," which, in his opinion, is already a local veneration.

In 1981, the Imperial Family were glorified by the Council of Bishops of the Russian Orthodox Church Outside of Russia (ROCOR). This event intensified attention to the question of the sanctity of the last Russian Tsar in the USSR as well.

In the second half of the 1980s, in connection with Perestroika, political activity increased in Soviet society, and it became possible to discuss the previously taboo topics. One of these issues was the canonization of the Imperial Family.

On the evening of 16th July 1989, people began to gather on the vacant lot where the Ipatiev House had previously stood. There, for the first time, public prayers to the Royal Martyrs were openly recited. On 18th August 1990, the first wooden cross was erected on the site of the Ipatiev House, near which believers began to pray once or twice a week and read akathists.

In the 1980s, Russia also raised the issue of the official canonization of at least the Tsar's five children, whose innocence is beyond doubt. Mention was made of icons painted without the blessing of the Church, and in which only they were depicted, without their parents. In 1992, the Empress's sister, Grand Duchess Elizabeth Feodorovna, another victim of the Bolsheviks, was canonized. Nevertheless, there were a large number of opponents of canonization.

Post-Soviet period

In 1993, "repentance for the sin of regicide on behalf of the entire Church" was offered by Patriarch Alexei II [1929-2008], who wrote: "We call upon all our people, all their children, regardless of their political views and views on history, regardless of their ethnic origin, religious affiliation, their attitude to the idea of monarchy and to the personality of the last Russian Emperor."

Churches, monasteries, memorial crosses and monuments

In the early 1990s, an Orthodox cross was erected at the site where the Imperial Family were murdered in Ekaterinburg. In 1991, Archbishop Melchizedek (Lebedev) blessed the installation of a memorial cross at Ganina Yama. A small chapel was built on Ascension Hill.

In 2000, during his visit to the Ural capital, Patriarch Alexei II blessed the creation of a monastery in honor of the Royal Passion-Bearers at Ganina Yama. The Monastery of the Holy Royal Passion-Bearers was established by 2001-2002. It has seven wooden churches, including the Church of the Holy Royal Passion-Bearers.

In May 1996, in the village of Taininskoye (Mytishchi), near the Church of the Annunciation of the Most Holy Theotokos, sculptor Vyacheslav Klykov (1939-2006) erected a monument to Nicholas II. On 1st April 1997, the monument was blown up by members of the left-wing extremist organization Revvoensovet (RVS). The sculptor called it sacrilege committed by the enemies of the Father-

land. In August 2000, the sculpture was restored and received the blessing of Patriarch Alexei II.

In October 2001, the State Duma considered a project to erect a monument to Nicholas II on Lubyanka Square in Moscow, but the proposal did not receive wide support.

Since the death and martyrdom of Nicholas II and his family, 24 churches, chapels and monasteries dedicated to the Holy Royal Martyrs have been constructed in Russia and abroad. Among the most notable is the Church on the Blood in the Name of All Russian Saints, built on the site of the Ipatiev House in Ekaterinburg (2003) and the Monastery of the Holy Royal Passion-Bearers, built at Ganina Yama near Ekaterinburg (2000). Many more churches, chapels and monasteries are planned for cities, towns and villages across the Russian Federation.

Religious processions and rallies. Tsar's Days

In July 1990, at one of the rallies of national-patriots, the murder of the Imperial Family was referred to as a "ritual," which was interpreted as "the symbolic destruction of the sovereignty of the Russian people."

In July 1989, about 200-250 people gathered at the site of the Ipatiev House, and in the early 1990s, several thousand people gathered together with the clergy of the Ekaterinburg diocese. The initiator of this movement was an activist first of the ROCOR and then of the Russian Orthodox Church, Alexander Markovich Verkhovsky [b. 1962], an associate of Archbishop Melchizedek (Lebedev), who took an active part in all the Orthodox rites on Ascension Hill.

It was on Ascension Hill in Ekaterinburg that Cross

A tall Orthodox cross marks the edge of the mine shaft - visible as a depression in the ground - where the remains of the Imperial Family were discarded after their brutal murder in the Ipatiev House

procession began. Since that time, a religious procession has been held in Ekaterinburg every year, ending at Ganina Yama. On 19th May 2001 [the anniversary of Nicholas II's birth], several thousand people took part in a 20 km Cross procession from the center of Ekaterinburg to Ganina Yama.

Every year since 2002, Ekaterinburg has hosted the Festival of Orthodox Culture - Tsar's Days, held on 16-17 July. The event is attended by Orthodox pilgrims from all over Russia. The main event of this festival culminates on the night of 16/17 July. An outdoor Divine Liturgy is performed outside the Church on the Blood, followed by a 21-kilometer penitential procession of the Royal Cross from the Church on the Blood to the Monastery of the Royal Passion-Bearers at Ganina Yama, repeating the path taken by the murdered Tsar and his family in the early morning hours of 17th July 1918.

In 2006, about 15,000 pilgrims took part in this procession, in 2007 - 20,000, in 2008 – up to 35,000, in 2012 - 50,000, in 2013 – about 40,000, in 2015 – over 60,000. In 2016, 50,000 to 80,000. The "Royal Procession" in Ekaterinburg brings pilgrims from different cities of Russia and abroad. In July 2015, a group of Japanese samurai participated in the event for the first time. In 2017, more than 60,000 believers took part in the Tsar's Days.

The largest number of participants, however, was in 2018 - the year marking the 100th anniversary of the death and martyrdom of the Imperial Family - an estimated 100,000 people took part, attracting pilgrims from dozens of foreign countries, including the USA, Canada, UK, among many others.

In 2019 - 60,000 took part, In 2020, 10 thousand people participated. The COVID pandemic hit Russia very hard, and thus had a negative impact on the number of participants - 10,000 in 2020, and 2,000 in 2021. In 2022 - 46,000 took part and in 2023 - the year marking the 300th anniversary of the founding of Ekaterinburg, some 40,000 pilgrims participated.

Religious processions related to the veneration of the Imperial Family also take place in the village of Taininskoye, a suburb of Moscow. On 17th July, 2013, up to 50,000 people took part in the procession.

Between 12th-17th July 2001, a large-scale "Royal Procession" in memory of the death and martyrdom of the Imperial Family took place along the Volga River to Kostroma. Organizers noted that this was done in the name of revival of Holy Russia. On 15th March 2007, about 100 St. Petersburg residents held a religious procession from St. Petersburg to Pskov in commemoration of the 90th anniversary of the abdication of Nicholas II in 1917. In 2008, on the anniversary of the 90th anniversary of the murder of the Imperial Family, religious processions and memorial services were held in the suburbs of St. Petersburg, Ryazan, Kiev, Odessa, Dnepropetrovsk, Rostov-on-Don, Tobolsk and Ulan-Ude. Since 2009, religious processions and prayer vigils have been regularly held in St. Petersburg, where they are attended by 500 to 1,000 believers. In July 2016, the International Youth Procession "The Tsar's Way" was held in St. Petersburg. In July 2012, a penitential procession was held in Samara, which gathered more than 500

people, and has been held every year since then.

Since 2001, the "Tsar's Days in Ivanovo" have been held annually in May, the participants of which believe that in 1917 there was not a change of power, but "the destruction of the God-ordained order of things".

In mid-June 1999, a procession of the cross was held in which the icon of Nicholas II and the icon of the Mother of God, were taken on an airplane and flown along the borders of Russia. A month later, several dozen believers carried the icon from Ivanovo to Kostroma. Since that time, processions with the participation of this icon have been regularly held in various across Russia.

On the anniversary of the death and martyrdom of the Imperial Family, Orthodox fundamentalists have held prayer vigils and religious processions in Moscow for several years, starting with the monument to Cyril and Methodius created by the sculptor Vyacheslav Klykov. At these events, the murder of the Imperial Family was referred to as a "ritual killing." The procession was organized jointly by the Union of Orthodox Banner Bearers, the Union of Christian Revival and the Union of Orthodox Brotherhood, headed by Leonid Simonovich-Niksic and Vladimir Osipov. In 2007, the event was held in the Church of All Saints on Sokol, where, under the slogan "Down with the regicides", the participants demanded the renaming of the Voykovskaya metro station on Moscow. In July 2016, an event was held by monarchist organizations in Moscow's Suvorov Square, where the struggle of Christ with the Antichrist and the "ritual murder" was commemorated, and Alexei Uchitel's controversial film *Matilda*, which was in production, was protested.

In June 2016, the participants of the religious procession "For Peace in Donbass", held on the initia-

Pilgrimage to Ganina Yama – "for reflection and prayer" - Paul Gilbert

tive of the Russian Public Movement "Common Cause", icons of the Holy Tsar-Martyr Nicholas II and the Holy Tsesarevich Alexei Nikolaevich were carried in the procession. The event was accompanied by sermons on the feat of the Holy Tsar and on the need to revive the monarchy.

In the early 2000s, the Zemshchina newspaper regularly published chronicles of religious processions and prayer vigils, at which the Russian tsars were remembered as "restraining" and the "mystery of lawlessness" identified with the activities of Jews and Freemasons was cursed. Such memory is cultivated by the Union of Orthodox Banner Bearers and the Christian Revival Union. Their amateur prayers for the restoration of autocracy. A joint prayer vigil dedicated to the 94th anniversary of the execution of the Imperial Family was held in July 2012 in Moscow in the park named after cosmonaut V.N. Volkov by the Christian Revival Union, the Union of Orthodox Brotherhoods and the Russian Imperial Movement. They jointly claim that the murder of the Tsar and his family had been committed by Jews at the behest of their brethren from the United States. More than 300 people took part in the event.

With the blessing of Metropolitan Vladimir of St. Petersburg and Ladoga, a penitential procession of the cross from St. Petersburg to Ekaterinburg - a journey of 1841 km [1144 miles] on foot - took place, and has been held every year since. It symbolizes repentance for the sin of the Russian people's apostasy from the 1613 conciliar oath of allegiance to the Romanov dynasty.

Iconography

There is both a collective image of the Imperial Family and each of its members individually. In "foreign" icons, the Imperial Family are joined by their faithful servants, who were ;ater canonized as passion-bearers or saints. Passion-bearers can be depicted both in contemporary clothes of the early 20th century, and in the Old Russian style robes, reminiscent in style of royal robes with parsun.

Figures of the Imperial Family are also found in the multi-figured icons "The Cathedral of the New Martyrs and Confessors of Russia" and "The Cathedral of the Holy Patrons of Hunters and Fishermen".

A number of Myrrh-streaming icons, depicting the image of the Holy Tsar-Martyr Nicholas II are today found in a number of churches in Russia: Myrrh-streaming icon in Butovo; the Nadym Icon of Tsar Nicholas II, revered as one of the main shrines of the Siberian Cossack Army of the Union of Cossacks of Russia; the Myrrh-streaming icon of the Tsar's Family in the Church of St. Nicholas the Wonderworker in Biryulyov; the myrrh-streaming icon of Emperor Nicholas II, owned by Oleg Belchenko, in the Church of St. Nicholas in Pyzhi, it travels regularly around Russia and abroad for important church events.

The first report of myrrh streaming from an icon of Nicholas II was on 7th November 1998, in the house of the writer A. V. Dyakova, before the canonization of the royal family.

Relics

Patriarch Alexei II, on the eve of the 2000 Council of Bishops, which performed the act of glorification of the Imperial Family, said of the remains found near Ekaterinburg: "We have doubts about the authenticity of the remains, and we cannot call on the faithful to venerate false relics if they are recognized as such in the future." Metropolitan Yuvenaly, referring to the judgment of the Holy

Synod of 26th February 1998, "The assessment of the reliability of scientific and investigative conclusions, as well as the testimony of their inviolability or irrefutability, is not within the competence of the Church. The scientific and historical responsibility for the conclusions made in the course of the investigation and study regarding the "Ekaterinburg remains" rests entirely with the Republican Center for Forensic Medical Research and the Prosecutor General's Office of the Russian Federation. The decision of the State Commission to identify the remains found near Ekaterinburg as belonging to Emperor Nicholas II and his family caused serious doubts and even confrontations in the Church and our society". In August 2000, the Council of Bishops stated that, "the 'Ekaterinburg remains' buried on 17th July 1998 in St. Petersburg cannot be recognized by us as those belonging to the Imperial Family."

Because of this position of the Moscow Patriarchate, which has not changed since then, the remains identified by the government commission as those belonging to Tsar Nicholas II and his family, who were buried in July 1998 in the Peter and Paul Cathedral are not venerated by the ROC as holy relics.

It is interesting to note that Nicholas II's hair, cut at the age of three, are venerated as relics.

Doctrine of the Tsar-Redeeming

Among some Orthodox monarchists, the doctrine of the Tsar-redeemer is widespread, according to which Nicholas II is identified with Christ as a "redeemer." Critics call this concept "the heresy of Tsarism." Historian and sociologist N. A. Mitrokhin believes that it is impossible to call the *"tsarebozhniki"* a sect, since it is an insulting name. He also notes that the sect seeks to distinguish itself into something independent; the researcher attributes the movement to cultism and the fundamentalist part of the Russian Orthodox Church.

Every year, in the days leading up to 18th July, billboards such as this are installed in cities across Russia. The inscription reads «Прости нас, Государь!» - «Forgive us, Sovereign!»

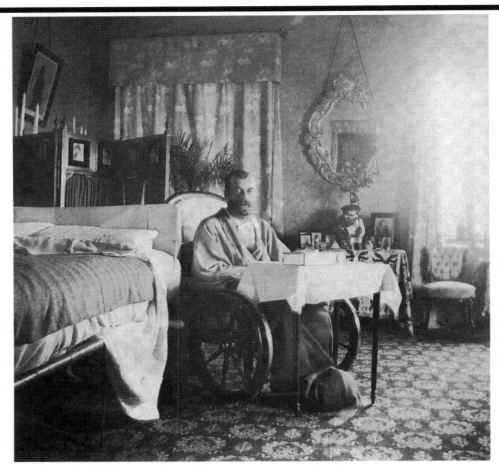

Emperor Nicholas II recovering from typhoid at Livadia, December 1900

Nicholas II's personal battle with typhoid in 1900

by Paul Gilbert

During Tsarist times, typhoid, or "spotted fever", affected every one from paupers to emperors—the often fatal illness did not discriminate. This intestinal infection caused by a specific type of Salmonella bacterium was a frequent guest in the imperial residences. And all because of poor sanitation. For example, the kitchen of the Winter Palace in St. Petersburg, only stopped taking water directly from the Neva River in 1868, while mineral filters and urns for boiling water were only in-

stalled in the palace in the 1920s! And we are talking here only of the water used by the Imperial Family: servants, valets, stokers and porters lived in, and bustled in and out of, the Winter Palace. The common folk and acquaintances that came to visit the Imperial Family in their tiny rooms had a very careless attitude to personal hygiene and as a result, the palace was teeming with lice, bedbugs, cockroaches and, of course, mice.

It is not surprising then that under these conditions that Empress Maria Alexandrovna, the spouse of Emperor Alexander II, their son Alexander Alexandrovich (future Alexander II) and the latter's daughter Xenia Alexandrovna all caught typhoid fever.

During his stay in Livadia[1] in the autumn of 1900, Nicholas II became gravely ill with typhoid. Initially, doctors were afraid to diagnose the disease for a long time and then they argued about what medication to prescribe.

The Emperor fell ill with what proved to be a rather serious from of typhoid. The Empress had a great horror of the illness, but a crisis always found her self-possessed and resourceful. She nursed the Emperor herself, even doing the night nursing, and acted as his private secretary when he was able to attend to papers, transmitting his decisions to his Ministers. The Empress wrote to her sister, Princess Louis [aka Victoria of Battenberg], at the time:

"Nicky really was an angel of patience during his wearisome illness, never complaining, always ready to do all one bid him. His old valet and I nursed him. The shock of his illness and feeling myself necessary gave me new strength, as I had been very wretched before. I rebelled at a nurse being taken and we managed perfectly ourselves."

Orchie [Alexandra's old nurse] would wash his face and hands in the morning. She would bring the Empress her meals, where she would take them while resting on the sofa in her husband's room. She suffered from head and heartache, the latter from nerves and many sleepless nights. When Nicholas began getting better, she read to him.

He first had a digestive upset on 22nd October 1900, and almost immediately the Emperor's temperature rose to 39-40 degrees Celsius (102-104 degrees Fahrenheit). The high temperature and severe headache, coupled with food poisoning, continued until 12th November.

The Emperor actually received no treatment. Despite being pregnant for the fourth time and in a lot of pain, Alexandra nursed him back to health, rarely leaving his side. While Alexandra Feodorovna was the one who looked after him, his sister Grand Duchess Xenia Alexandrovna, recorded her brother's illness and recovery:

"Poor Nicky is lying in bed, he didn't sleep at all at night because of terrible pains in his back. In the morning his temperature was 38.2 – during the day 38.7. His eyes are tired and pale! [Dr.] Girsh says that it's influenza! Thank God there's nothing in the lungs, or in general anywhere else. Poor Alix [Alexandra Feodorovna] – she looks very tired." – Xenia's diary, 27th October 1900

"Later on I drove to Livadia and looked in on Nicky for a minute. The back of his neck hurts terribly, and he doesn't know where to turn his head. All the pain from his back and legs has gone upwards, and he is suffering terribly. Poor Alix has forgotten about her own sickness and is moving around more. Girsh is adamant, that it isn't typhoid (we asked him). Girsh asked Nicky to call someone else, to put everyone's mind at rest – it was decided to call for [Dr.] Tikhonov." – Xenia's diary, 29th October 1900

"We met Tikhonov, who told us that several symptoms of typhoid had developed, and that they were almost sure that it was typhoid! At Livadia we immediately questioned Girsh. It's astounding that influenza should suddenly turn into typhoid!

"At Livadia we immediately questioned Girsh. It's

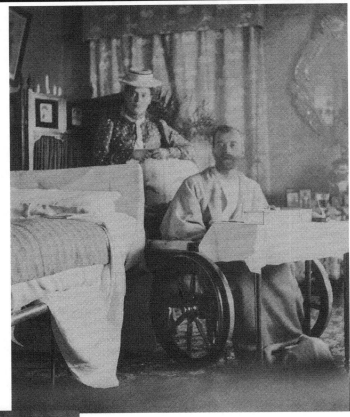

Grand Duchess Xenia Alexandrovna visits her brother Emperor Nicholas II, who is recovering from typhoid fever. Livadia, Crimea. December 1900

Empress Alexandra Feodorovna standing behind her husband, who is seated in a wheelchair while recovering from typhoid.

Nicholas II is seated in front of a table, wearing a dressing gown, and a rug placed over his legs. Livadia, Crimea. December 1900

astounding that influenza should suddenly turn into typhoid! With Alix's permission Professor Popov was sent for; we had lunch alone together downstairs; a little later [Count] Fredericks arrived, tearing his hair and saying he was in a terrible position, that everyone wanted news, while he was not allowed to tell anyone anything. He wanted us to persuade Alix to allow a bulletin to be published, which we were able to do. She agreed that there is nothing worse than trying to conceal things! We telegraphed poor Mama. Thank God Alix is so calm." – Xenia's diary, 31st October 1900

"Thank the Lord, Nicky had an excellent night – he slept until morning, his temperature was 38.7 and he felt well. Alix called me to see Nicky – he was in remarkably good spirits, and chatted and joked. Alix was also in a good mood, having slept well. They didn't want to let me go, but in the end I left of my own accord, as he needs complete rest and had been talking to much.

"All the unnecessary furniture has been removed from the bedroom, and will be taken into Alix's drawing room this afternoon. Alix is now sleeping in another bed, at least the doctors have achieved that much." – Xenia's diary, 1st November 1900

"They are not happy that Nicky's temperature is so low 36°, but the pulse is good at 66. They are afraid of a haemorrhage, God preserve us! It's so terrifying, help us God, save our Nicky!" – 13th November 1900

Against this background, discussions about who should succeed Nicholas II, in the event that he should die. The Empress attempted to persuade her husband to change the Laws of Succession to allow females to inherit the throne in the absence of any male heirs in order for their four-year-old daughter Grand Duchess Olga Nikolaevna [2] to inherit the empire, as opposed to her uncle, Grand Duke Michael Alexandrovich. Ultimately, these changes did not take place.

After 13th November, the Tsar's temperature started coming down and on 30th November, for the first time, Nicholas spent half an hour on his balcony. "It was sunny, warm and still... Thank God my typhoid was mild and I didn't suffer at all during the whole time. I had a strong appetite and now my weight is increasing noticeably every day..."

Nicholas recovered six months later, in May-June 1901, however, little Olga came down with typhoid. Alexandra would nurse their eldest daughter through her illness.

On the 24th November 1900 Nicholas wrote to his mother:

"About my little wife I can only say that she was my guardian angel, looked after me better than any sister of mercy!"

NOTES:

[1] Up until 1911, Nicholas II and his family stayed in the Small Livadia Palace during their visits to Crimea, after which they lived in the iconic white stone palace, which was constructed on the site of the Large Livadia Palace. The Small Palace survived until the Great Patriotic War (1941-45).

[2] The Succession Prospects of Grand Duchess Olga Nikolaevna (1895-1918) by Carolyn Harris, published in Canadian Slavic Papers, Volume 54, 2012 – Issue 1-2

Nicholas II records his memories of *Pascha* (Easter)

by Paul Gilbert

Christ is risen! With these words, the hearts of all Orthodox Christians are filled with a feeling of ineffable joy and spiritual warmth. The same was true for the Russian Imperial Family, which is now a family of saints. They endured a great deal, but in all periods of their lives we see that they unwaveringly followed the Lord and managed to preserve the light of faith. Tsar Nicholas's diaries enlighten us as to how they spent this holy day.

The Pascha of 1895 was the first for the newly wedded couple. Tsar Alexander III had died in the autumn of 1894, whereupon his son Nicholas, ascended the Russian throne and married the German princess Alice in November 1894. The young emperor was on the threshold of a different life. A new page of Russian history was unfolding.

In 1895, Nicholas II writes in his diary about his first Pascha as husband and Emperor, and in subsequent years:

1st April Saturday

It significantly froze tonight, though the day was sunny. I have not sensed such freedom for a long time, as today I did not have any reports and had nothing sent to me for reading. We went to the Liturgy at 11:30. <…> Alix set about coloring eggs with Misha [Grand Duke Mikhail] and Olga [Grand Duchess]. We all sat down to dinner at 8 o'clock. Presents and various surprises for one another in the eggs came in the evening. At 11:50 we headed for Paschal Matins, which was celebrated in our home church for the first time.

2nd April, Sunday

The service ended at 1:45. We broke the Lenten fast at Mama's: Alix, Xenia [Grand Duchess], Sandro [Grand Duke Alexander Mikhailovich] and uncle Alexei [Grand Duke Alexei Alexandrovich]. We slept until 9 o'clock in the morning. I had to deal with the eggs—that was a burdensome and fatiguing waste of time. Alix was distributing the gifts. At breakfast were uncle Vladimir [Grand Duke Vladimir Alexandrovich] and aunt Miechen [Grand Duchess Maria Pavlovna the elder] with the children, and George. We set out to pay visits to the entire family. The day was bright, though cold. We drank tea at home. Alix was so exhausted that she did not go to the Vigil service. We had supper at 8 o'clock. I devoted myself to reading, as usual.

1896

21st March, Thursday

The girls received Holy Communion at the Liturgy. Ours was perfectly serene, but Irina [Grand Duchess Irina Alexandrovna] cried a little. <...> The Service of the Twelve Passion Gospels lasted 1 1/2 h.

23rd March, Saturday

We attended the Liturgy at 11:30. After it was over, we had breakfast at Xenia's place. She did not feel well and did not attend Paschal Matins, which was a pity! Benckendorff and I were sorting the eggs of glass and porcelain. <...> We set out for the Bolshaya Church at 11:45. Before the Liturgy began, I greeted 288 people. We came back to the Malachite [room] at 2:30 to break the fast.

24th March, Bright Sunday

We went to bed at about four o'clock, when the dawn was breaking. We got up by 8:30. Finally, the morning was free from all business. Khristosovanie [the Paschal triple kiss] with all the people began at 11:30 in the Malachite room; nearly five hundred people received eggs. <...> We set about paying visits to the whole family; we saw aunt Sany [Grand Duchess Alexandra Josiphovna]. After taking a horse ride along the embankment, we came back home by teatime. I did some reading after we bathed our daughter. At 7:15 we went to the Vigil service; we had dinner with uncle Misha afterward at Xenia and Sandro's place. We gave her our presents. We took another ride to breathe some fresh air.

The year of 1905 was one of the most troublesome for Russia. It had already waged war with Japan, and was then hit by the storm of a revolution that was to be a forerunner of the imminent catastrophe. The Imperial Family was together anyway, supporting one another and praying to Lord for intercession.

1905

14th April, Great Thursday

In the morning, we all received Holy Communion. Our Little Treasure behaved decently at the church. Then we took a walk. The weather was wonderful; the sun was burning fiercely. <...>

17th April, the Bright Resurrection of Christ

We got up at about 10 o'clock in the scorching morning. I had been greeting nearly six hundred people for an hour. We had breakfast at its time. It rained. <...> The weather was perfect. I was reading. A 7:00 we went to the Vigil service.

9-го Апрѣля 1900 года.

Болѣе чѣмъ когда-либо Первопрестольная нынѣ подтверждаетъ сказанное о ней незабвеннымъ Императоромъ Александромъ III: «Москва—храмъ всея Руси, а Кремль—алтарь этого храма...»

Благочестивѣйшіе ЦАРЬ и ЦАРИЦА говѣли и сподобились пріобщиться Св. Тайнъ у того самаго «Спаса за золотой рѣшеткой», гдѣ говѣли и причащались первые державные предки нынѣ благополучно Царствующаго Дома. Подъ сѣнію древнихъ Святынь Московскихъ какъ бы обновилась и вновь процвѣла родная старина. Отъ лѣтъ древнихъ, свидѣтелемъ которыхъ стоитъ Кремль златоверхій, живы завѣты Святой Руси и въ настоящихъ событіяхъ получаютъ новую опору и утвержденіе. Православный народъ видитъ во-очію, что у него съ своимъ ЦАРЕМЪ-Батюшкой единый Богъ, едина вѣра, едина совѣсть и едина правда. На этомъ духовномъ единеніи ЦАРЯ съ народомъ выросла и окрѣпла Держава Русская, въ этомъ единеніи ея сила и величіе, залогъ преуспѣянія.

Торжественно загудѣлъ Иванъ-Великій, властно раздается его мощный зовъ въ прозрачномъ сумракѣ пасхальной ночи, и всѣ сорокъ сороковъ Московскихъ церквей послушно отвѣчаютъ ему краснымъ звономъ, который гулко переливается по Бѣлокаменной съ благою радостною вѣстью: ХРИСТОСЪ ВОСКРЕСЕ!

И Кремль съ его золотыми маковками, и все окрестъ его залито моремъ праздничныхъ огней. Какъ бы ожили и движутся святыя Кремлевскія высоты въ этомъ чудномъ сліяніи звуковъ и свѣта — то знаменитый пасхальный крестный ходъ, золотой волной раздвигающійся по Кремлю... И во главѣ этого несмѣтнаго сонма русскихъ людей всякаго званія и чина, преисполненныхъ восторга и умиленія, шествуютъ ЦАРЬ и ЦАРИЦА, осѣняемые безчисленнымъ множествомъ хоругвей, крестовъ, иконъ и окруженные плотною стѣною беззавѣтной любви и преданности народной. Единымъ сердцемъ, едиными устами обмѣнивается Царственная Чета со всей великой русской семьей благостными привѣтствіями:

ХРИСТОСЪ ВОСКРЕСЕ!— ВО ИСТИНУ ВОСКРЕСЕ!

1906

30th March, Great Thursday,

In the morning, we and all the children received the Holy Communion. Spiritual comfort embraced me for some hours. The Matins of the Twelve Passion Gospels lasted from 7 till 8:40.

2nd April, the Bright Resurrection of Christ

The Matins began early, at midnight. I greeted the Tsarskoye Selo garrison, including the officers. The service ended at 2:30. We came back home to break the fast at a family dinner. I slept soundly until 10. The morning was sunny, but later it started to rain. A large khristosovanie went from 11:30 till 12:45, I greeted over six hundred people. I took a stroll after breakfast. The weather got better by 4 o'clock in the afternoon, though it got a bit cooler. At 7:30 we went to the Vigil service. <...>

1907

21st April, the Bright Resurrection of Christ

The Matins began at 12, and the Liturgy was over at 2:15. After coming back home, we broke the fast in the Round Hall. We slept until 9:30. It was pouring rain the whole morning; the weather was chilly. I greeted seven hundred people. We listened to three numbers that the choir sang to us. We had a family breakfast. I took a stroll with Dmitry [probably Grand Duke Dmitry Pavlovich] and broke the ice in the pond. The weather got better. I was

Photo on opposite page: Commemorative leaflet depicting Emperor Nicholas II and Empress Alexandra Feodorovna attending the Easter service in the Moscow Kremlin, 9th April 1900

reading. We went to the Vigil service at 7:30. <...>

1908

11th April, Great Thursday

At 9 o'clock we came to the Liturgy in the cave church and received the Holy Communion. We returned home at 11.

I took a walk after having some tea.

The day was radiant. All the bushes are beginning to show green buds. After breakfast the children and I broke the last blocks of ice. We had tea a bit earlier, at 4, and at 6 o'clock we headed for the Matins of the Twelve Gospels. It was in the Main church. We sat to dinner at 8:15. I devoted a lot of time to reading aloud afterward.

12th April, Friday

I had almost no work to do in the morning and took a little boat trip with Maria and Anastasia around our pond. At 2 o'clock we all went to the Vespers and came back home at 3:30. <...>

13th April, Saturday

I woke up at 4:15 in the morning; by 5 o'clock I was at the Matins in the regiment church with Olga, Tatiana and Maria. The procession around the church at a magnificent dawn reminded me of Moscow, the Dormition Cathedral and the same service! We went home on foot and arrived at 6. I slept until 9:30. Had a walk. We all went to the Liturgy, which was over at one o'clock in the afternoon. <...> The children were coloring eggs with the yacht officers. I was reading until 8 o'clock. We gave presents to one another. At 11:30 we set out to the church for the Midnight Office. This was the

Early 20th century postcard depicting Nicholas II presents an egg to one of his soldiers during Pascha

first service for Alexei, he went back home with Anastasia after the Matins.

The service in our nice church was festive and marvelously beautiful. <...> We returned home at 2.

We broke the fast with the elder daughters.

14th April, Pascha

I went to bed at 3:30 and got up 9:30.

The morning was gray, but the sun came out in the afternoon. The Khristosovanie took place before breakfast; I greeted 720 people. <...>

Then the First World War ensued. It was most tragic for the Russian nation—the country lost millions of people and moved closer to the revolution.

1914

6th April, the Bright Resurrection of Christ

I greeted everyone in the church after the Matins. The Liturgy was over at 1:45, and we went to the dining room to break the fast. We came home at about 3. I slept until 9 o'clock. <...> Khristosovanie began downstairs at 11:30, 512 people. The whole family was together at breakfast. Alix was tired and lay down to have some rest until 5. I walked with the children and the officers to the Krestovaya hill in Oreanda, where we sat for a while and had some rest, admiring the view. We drank tea with a delicious paskha, butter and milk. I answered telegrams. The Vespers was at 7:30. <...>

1915

19th April, Great Thursday

We all received Holy Communion. Alexei had to commune after the Liturgy lying in bed, since he had swollen lymph nodes. I went for a walk after drinking tea in his playroom. <...> Received Count Friederichs at 6 and went to the Matins of the Twelve Gospels, which was over at 8:15. I was reading for the entire evening.

22nd April, the Bright Resurrection of Christ

The cathedral was beautifully lit by sparklers during the procession. It was slightly cold; the night was cloudless.

The Liturgy ended at 2 o'clock. We had festive dinner with all the daughters. I slept until 9:30. The day was sunny and bright. I greeted the court from 11 till 12:30. After breakfast I had a long walk and worked. <...>

1916

7th April 7, Great Thursday

A very tough day. I went to the Liturgy at 9:20, where Alexeyev and many staff officers received the Holy Communion. Took a walk in the garden and listened to a report at 11. Few people were at breakfast and dinner. I was reading. I took a car ride along the Gomel highway and a stroll at the same place; I had walked with Alix and the children where we had made a fire. The Matins of the Twelve Gospels took an hour and a half. I devoted the evening to the work.

8th April 8, Friday

The twenty-second anniversary of our engagement, the second year that we have not spend this day together. <...>

10th April, the Bright Resurrection of Christ

The Liturgy ended at 1:50. They all came to my place, I greeted everyone and we broke the fast. The night was chilly and cloudless. I slept until 9:30. In an hour began khristosovanie with the staff, the managers, the clergy, the police and the locals of higher ranks.

Pascha of 1917 was preceded by the February revolution that struck the country nearly two months before, and the air of revolution and disaster permeated the Tsar's journal entries. On March 2, Tsar Nicholas was forced to abdicate the throne and celebrated the holy feast as the ordinary "Colonel Romanov". The entire family was together, as usual.

1917

30th March, Great Thursday

<...> At 10 o'clock we went to the Liturgy, where many of our people received Holy Communion. I took a short stroll with Tatiana. Today the 'victims of the revolution' were buried in our park, in front of the middle of the Alexander Palace. We could hear the sounds of a funeral march and "La Marseillaise". Everything was over by 5:30. At 6 o'clock we went to the Matins of the Twelve Gospels. <...>

2nd April, the Bright Resurrection of Christ

The Matins and Liturgy ended at 1:40. We broke the fast altogether; there sixteen of us. I did not go to bed soon as I had eaten substantially. I got up at about 10. The day was bright and truly festive. I took a short walk in the morning. I greeted all the servants before breakfast, and Alix gave out porcelain eggs that we had managed to keep from past reserves. Overall, there were 135 people. <...> Alexei and Anastasia went outdoors for the first time. <...>

3rd April, Monday

A wonderful spring day. <...> I went to the Liturgy with Tatiana and Anastasia at 11 o'clock. After breakfast we went out to the park with Alexei, I was breaking ice for the whole time by our summer embankment <...>.

In 1918, the Romanov family was separated; the Tsar, Alexandra Feodorovna and Maria we're transferred to Yekaterinburg, while the rest of the children remained in the Siberian town of Tobolsk. Some three months before the notorious murder, that Pascha was the last in their lives.

1918

19th April, Great Thursday,

The day was beautiful, windy, dust was rushing around the town and the sun was shining brightly, penetrating through the windows. In the morning I was reading the book La Sagasse et la destinée to Alix. Later I continued to read the Bible. The breakfast was served late, at 2 o'clock in the afternoon. Then we were allowed to go out to the garden for an hour, and we all, except Alix, took the opportunity. The weather turned cooler, some drops of rain fell upon the earth. It was pleasant to breathe some fresh air. When the bells rang, a sense of sadness imbued me—it is now Passion Week, and we are deprived of any possibility to attend its magnificent services, and moreover, cannot observe the fast! I had the joy of bath before tea. Dinner was served at 9. In the evening we, all the people dwelling in the four rooms, gathered in the hall, where Botkin read aloud the twelve Gospels. We all went to bed afterward.

21st April, Great Saturday

I woke up quite late; the day was grey, cold, with snowstorms. I spent the whole morning reading, writing a couple of lines in each letter from Alix and Maria to the daughters, and drawing a plan of this [Ipatiev] house. We had lunch at 1:30. At Botkin's request, a priest and a deacon were allowed to come to our place at 8 o'clock. They served the Matins quickly and well. It was a great comfort to pray in such an atmosphere and hear "Christ is

Risen!' Ukraintsev, the commandant's assistant, and the soldiers of the watch were present. We had dinner after the service and went to bed early.

22nd April, the Bright Resurrection of Christ

For the whole evening and partly in the night we could hear cracks of fireworks that people set off in the different parts of the city. It was 3° c. in the afternoon, and the weather was grey. We greeted one other at tea and ate kulichi and eggs; we failed to get paskhas.

We had lunch and dinner at their respective times. We took a half an hour stroll. In the evening we spent a lot of time talking to Ukraintsev at Botkin's place.

Emperor Nicholas II, Empress Alexandra Feodorovna and their daughter Grand Duchess Maria Nikolaevna

On this day - 26th (O.S. 13th) April 1918
Nicholas II makes his final journey

by Paul Gilbert

Today – 26th (O.S. 13th) April 1918 – marks the 106th anniversary of the transfer of members of the Russian Imperial Family from Tobolsk to Ekaterinburg. It was on this day, that they embarked on their final journey to Golgotha.

Emperor Nicholas II, Empress Alexandra Feodorovna, along with their daughter Grand

Duchess Maria Nikolaevna departed Tobolsk for Ekaterinburg. They were accompanied by several members of their retinue. Together, they would be imprisoned in the Ipatiev House, and subsequently murdered in the early morning hours of 17th July 1918. There were no survivors.

In the early morning hours of 26th (O.S. 13th) April

1918 they departed Tobolsk under the escort of Vasily Yakovlev's detachment, which comprised of a convoy of nineteen tarantasses (four-wheeled carriages). Yakovlev was acting on order from the Bolshevik leadership to "deliver Nicholas II to the red capital of the Urals" – Ekaterinburg.

As Tsesarevich Alexei Nikolaevich was very ill, he remained in Tobolsk, with his three sisters Grand Duchesses Olga, Tatiana and Anastasia, as well as Pierre Gilliard, Charles Sydney Gibbes and other members of the family's retinue. They reunited with their parents and sister in Ekaterinburg the following month.

From the diary of the Tsar that day: "At 4 o'clock in the morning we said goodbye to our dear children and climbed into the tarantases. The weather was cold, with an unpleasant wind, the road was very rough with terrible jolts from a seized-up wheel."

Cross procession in memory of the Holy Royal Martyrs held in Ekaterinburg

On 30th April 2024, a Cross Procession along the "Path of Sorrows" honouring the memory of Emperor Nicholas II, Empress Alexandra Feodorovna, and their daughter Grand Duchess Maria Nikolaevna was held in Ekaterinburg. The day marked the 106th anniversary of their arrival in the Ural capital from Tobolsk.

Accompanying them were a number of servants: Dr. Evgeny (Eugene) Sergeyevich Botkin, Prince Vasily Alexandrovich Dolgorukov, maid Anna Stepanovna Demidova, valet Terentiy Ivanovich Chemodurov and boatswain Ivan Dmitrievich Sednev.

Every year on this day, the Ekaterinburg Diocese prayerfully celebrate the memory of the Holy Royal Martyrs. In churches, prayers are made to the Holy Imperial Family, and people also honour them by taking part in the Cross Procession along the "Ekaterinburg's Path of Sorrow", to the places associated with them on the day of their arrival in

A very sad photo . . . the tarantasses which transported Emperor Nicholas II, Empress Alexandra Feodorovna and Grand Duchess Maria Nikolaevna from Tobolsk to Tyumen, and then by train to Ekaterinburg. This photo was hastily shot by Charles Sydney Gibbes from the window of the Governor's Mansion on the morning of 26th (O.S. 13th) April 1918.

the Ural capital.

The clergy of the Ekaterinburg Diocese lead the Cross Procession along the "Ekaterinburg Cross Procession", they are joined by Orthodox Christians, monarchists and other adherent's to the last Tsar and his family. Together they prayfully walk the Path of Sorrows, walking in the footsteps of the Tsar, his family and their faithful servants, expressing their love and reverence for them.

The "Ekaterinburg Path of Sorrows" begin at the place where Emperor Nicholas II, Empress Alexandra Feodorovna and Grand Duchess Maria Nikolaevna disembarked from the train on 30th April 1918. Here, near the Shartash Railway Station (in 1918 – Yekaterinburg-II Station), a Memorial Cross and foundation stone were installed. A church in honour of the Valaam Icon of the Mother of God, one of the three miraculous icons that appeared during the reign of Nicholas II, will be constructed on this site.

The Cross Procession then proceeds along Vostochnaya Street, where the Church of the Icon of the Mother of God "Port Arthur" was erected at the intersection with Shevchenko Street. Here, according to the historical version, on 23rd May 1918, Tsesarevich Alexei Nikolaevich, Grand Duchesses Olga, Tatiana and Anastasia Nikolaevna arrived by

"Transfer of the Romanov family to the Ural Soviet". 1927. Artist Vladimir Nikolaevich Pchelin (1869-1941). From the Collection of the Sverdlovsk Regional Museum of Local Lore in Ekaterinburg.

A Cross Procession is held every year in the Ural capital, marking the arrival of Emperor Nicholas II, Empress Alexandra Feodorovna, Grand Duchess Maria Nikolaevna and their retainers from Tobolsk in April 1918.

train, placed under arrest, and then taken to the Ipatiev's House.

In 2008, a memorial stone was laid at the site, and in 2017, the construction of the Church of the Icon of the Mother of God "Port Arthur" was completed, the consecration of the church was performed by Metropolitan Kirill of Yekaterinburg and Verkhoturye.

Not far from the railway station, in Nevyansky Lane, stands the Church in Honour of the Reigning Icon of the Mother of God. It was consecrated in 2011 by Metropolitan Kirill of Yekaterinburg and Verkhoturye. In 1918, the Yekaterinburg-I Station was located here, and it was here on 30th April 1918, that the train carrying the Tsar, his family and their servants stood for several hours. An angry

mob had gathered at the station, forcing the train to travel to the Yekaterinburg-II Station.

he Cross Procession along the Path of Sorrows ends at the Church on the Blood on Tsarskaya Street. The Memorial Church was constructed on the site of the Ipatiev House, demolished in 1977. It was here, in the early morning hours of 17tj July 1918, that the Imperial Family and four faithful servants met their violent deaths at the hands of a firing squad and their martyrdom. Situted in the Lower Church there is the "Tsar's Room" aka as "The Imperial Room" – the altar of the side-chapel in honour of the Holy Royal Martyrs, which was erected on the site of the murder room, with the blessing of Metropolitan Kirill of Yekaterinburg and Verkhoturye for the Tsar's Days 2018.

The remains of Nicholas II, his wife, three of their children and their four faithful retainers were buried under the "sleepers bridge" at Porosenkov Log by their murderers in 1918

Nicholas II's grave was an "open secret" in 1920s Soviet Russia

by Paul Gilbert

"We hid them so well that the world will never find them," boasted Commissar for Supply in the Ural Region Soviet Pyotr Lazarevich Voykov (1888-1927), on the location of the murdered remains of Emperor Nicholas II and his family.

While the burial site of the Imperial Family at Porosenkov Log remained a secret to the world for more than 60 years, it was in fact an "open secret"[1] to a select few in the Soviet Union in the 1920s.

In January 1928 – ten years after the murders of Emperor Nicholas II, his family and four faithful retainers – the famous Soviet poet Vladimir Vladimirovich Mayakovsky (1893-1930) visited Sverdlovsk. It was at the city's Business Club that he met the Chairman of the Ekaterinburg City Executive Committee Anatoly Ivanovich Paramonov (1891-1970), making enquiries about the city and the last days of the Imperial Family.

Paramonov took Mayakovsky to the Ipatiev House, and then in minus 30-degree frost, along the Old Koptyaki Road to the place where the remains of the Imperial Family had been buried by their murderers – members of the Ural Soviet on 17th July 1918.

"Of course, it was nothing special – to see the grave of the tsar. In fact, nothing is visible there. It is very difficult to find as there are no signs or marks, this secret place is familiar only to a certain group of people," Mayakovsky wrote in his diary.

Three months after his trip to the Urals, Mayakovsky wrote the mockingly pathetic poem The Emperor, which indicated the place of burial with absolute toponymic accuracy. In his poem, Mayakovsky reveals clues: "Beyond the Iset [river], where the wind howled, the executive committee coachman fell silent and stood at the ninth verst."[2] "Beyond Iset at the ninth verst" is a key clue that indicated where to look for the tsar's grave on the Old Koptyaki Road. The poem further notes: "Here the cedar was torn with an ax, notches under the root of the bark, at the root, under the cedar, there is a road, and in it the emperor is buried."

The Emperor was published in the Soviet literary magazine Krasnaya Nov on 4th April 1928. Mayakovsky's poem made a terrible impression on the Russian/Soviet poet Marina Ivanovna Tsvetaeva (1892-1941). She deplored Mayakovsky's justification of the terrible massacre, as a kind of verdict of history. She insisted that the poet should be on the side of the victims, not the executioners, and if the story is cruel and unfair, he must speak against it. In 1929, in response, she began working on a poem about the Tsar's Family entitled Heart and Stone.

Mayakovsky's poem, as well as other evidence such as the "Yurovsky note", helped Soviet and Russian geologist Alexander Nikolayevich Avdonin and Soviet writer and filmmaker Geliy Trofimovich Ryabov (1932-2015) locate the remains of the Imperial Family in 1979[3].

In 1926, Mayakovsky visited Voykov in Warsaw, where the latter served as Soviet Ambassador to Poland. It was during this visit that Voykov told Mayakovsky about the regicide which took place in Ekaterinburg. Voykov was assassinated in Warsaw on 7th June 1927, by Boris Sofronovich Kowerda (1907-1987) a White émigré and monarchist. Kowerda planned to kill Voykov in order to "Avenge Russia, and the deaths of millions of people", as well for Voykov's participation in the decision to execute Nicholas II and his family.

Declassified photographs taken by members of the firing squad, as well as those who did not participate in the regicide, but who knew of the location of burial site, aided Paramonov and Mayakovsky to locate the "sleepers bridge" (see photo below).

The murderer Pyotr Zakharovich Ermakov (1884-1952) used a Mauser pistol[4], during the liquidation of the Imperial Family in the basement of the Ipatiev House. He brought it with him to the place where the bodies lay so that he could be photographed (see photo below).

"In the first half of the 1960s, one of the sons of the murderers applied to the Central Committee of the Communist Party with a letter addressed to the First Secretary of the Communist Party of the Soviet Union Nikita Sergeevich Khrushchev (1894-1971), boasting that his father had participated in the murder of the Imperial Family. He presented Khrushchev with two pistols that he had preserved: one for the Soviet leader, the other – to be

Vladimir Mayakovsky and Anatoly Paramonov

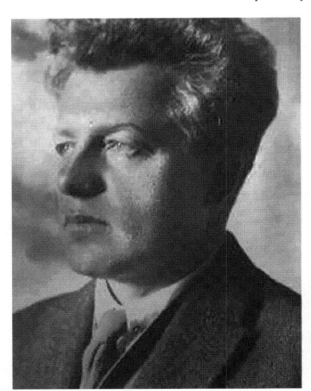

Pyotr Voykov and Boris Kowerda

handed over to Cuban revolutionary Fidel Castro (1926-2016) as the leader of the world revolution. At that time, documents in all the archives were still sealed, yet two of the executioners were still alive. And for history, the Radio Committee recorded their memories, which had been preserved and "coincided with those of Yakov Mikhailovich Yurovsky" (1878-1938), said Sergei Mironenko, Director of the State Archives of the Russian Federation [GARF} in Moscow.

Yurovsky served as commandant of the "House of Special Purpose" [Ipatiev House], and the chief executioner of the Tsar and his family. But his memories raised a lot of questions – some historians believe that the typewritten text may have been specially falsified by the GPU-NKVD-KGB, in order to send future search efforts on the wrong track, or a story written by a third party, such as the Soviet historian Mikhail Nikolayevich Pokrovsky[5].

According to Vladimir Nikolaevich Solovyov, senior investigator and forensic expert at the Main Department of Criminalistics (Forensic Center) of the Investigative Committee of the Russian Federation, who from 1991 to 2015 led the investigation into the death of the imperial family, "the real breakthrough was made quite recently".

Shortly after the completion of the work of the government commission, a safe was discovered in another archive, not in the State Archive, but in the former Central Party Archive, which had not been opened for many decades. It contained a manuscript of the famous Soviet historian Mikhail Nikolayevich Pokrovsky (1868-1932), a typewritten copy of which is kept in the State Archive. The discovery immediately confirmed that this is Yurovsky's recollection, recorded by Pokrovsky. According to Sergei Mironenko, the bottom of the last page of the manuscript had been torn off. Apparently, it contained the name of the place where the bodies were hidden. So there is no evidence? There is! As shown by the graphological examination, handwritten by Pokrovsky and Yurovsky, the name was entered into the typewritten version, the authenticity of which is considered beyond any doubt.

"Interestingly, at the end of the classic text of Yurovsky's note, there is an addition, made in pencil, which precisely indicates the place where the bodies were found," said Solovyov.

There has always been a mystique behind this story. A 1991 diagram clearly shows the location of the bodies. Their remains were not laid, but simply dumped by their murderers. For example, Olga's skull is under the skeleton of her father. But even in the photo of the burial site, opened in 1991, a telephone cable is clearly visible. When laying it, the cutter even cut off the arm of one of the skeletons. But how could the Soviet telephone technicians know where they were laying the cable, because even if they had read Mayakovsky's poem, the instructions were too obscure for them to link it to the burial site.

One more detail – small but important. According to Mayakovsky's poem, he wrote about "the cedar was torn with an axe". During a comprehensive survey of the area, a fallen stump, clearly cut long ago with an axe was found.

NOTES

[1] An "open secret" is a concept or idea that is "officially" secret or restricted in knowledge, but in practice (de facto) may be widely known; or it refers to something that is widely known to be true but which none of the people most intimately concerned are willing to categorically acknowl-

edge in public.

[2] A verst is a Russian measure of length, about 0.66 mile (1.1 km).

[3] The remains of the Imperial Family were first discarded at the Four Brothers Mine, which is today the site of the Monastery of the Holy Royal Martyrs at Ganina Yama. Avdonin and Ryabov discovered the second grave 3.8 km down the highway at Porosenkov Log.

[4] Yermakov's revolver can be seen on display in the Romanov Memorial Hall, located on the top floor of the Museum of History and Archaeology of the Urals, in Ekaterinburg

[5] Pokrovsky was a Russian Marxist historian, Bolshevik revolutionary and a public and political figure. One of the earliest professionally trained historians to join the Russian revolutionary movement, Pokrovsky is regarded as the most influential Soviet historian of the 1920s.

His attitude to the tsar, the nobility, generals, statesmen and church leaders and diplomats of the Tsarist period appear in the Pokrovsky's works in a completely different light – as selfish, cruel,

PHOTOS ON OPPOSITE PAGE:

Top photo: in the 1920s, the murderer Pyotr Zakharovich Yermakov returned to Porosenkov Log. On the reverse of this photo, he wrote: "I am standing on the grave of the Tsar".

Lower photo: Pyotr Zakharovich Yermakov (far right) posing with a group of prominent Ural Bolsheviks on the Tsar's grave[6], his Mauser pistol can be seen in the foreground in front of P.M. Bykov, author of The Last Days of Tsardom (1934).

limited, ignorant individuals. To achieve greater impact on the reader, representatives of the ruling classes and leaders were denounced with the help of satire, irony and grotesque. Thus, Pokrovsky's negative assessment of the reign of Nicholas II was accepted as the standard in the Soviet Union, where he was vilified.

[6] Group of prominent Ural Bolsheviks, photographed at the "grave of the Romanovs", 1924. This photo is on display in the Romanov Memorial Hall, located on the top floor of the Museum of History and Archaeology of the Urals, in Ekaterinburg

(from left to right): back row – A.I. Paramonov (chairman of the board of Uralselkhozbank and editor of Krestyanskaya Gazeta, *NN, M.M. Kharitonov (first secretary of the Ural regional committee of the RCP (b)), B.V. Didkovsky (deputy chairman of Uralplan), I.P. Rumyantsev (head of propaganda department), *NN, A.L. Borchaninov (chairman of the Tyumen regional executive committee); front row – D.E.Sulimov (chairman of the Ural regional executive committee), G.S. Moroz (head of the Yekaterinburg department of the GPU), M.V. Vasiliev (employee of Uralselkhozbank), P.M.Bykov (editor of the newspaper "Uralskaya Nov"), A.G. Kabanov, P.Z.Ermakov (employee of the Cheka)

*NN denotes "unknown identity"

New bust-monument of Nicholas II, installed in Zaplavnoye on 18th May 2024

Two new bust-monuments of Nicholas II Installed in Russia

by Paul Gilbert

In May 2024, two new bust-monuments were installed in the Russian Federation.

18th May - Zaplavnoye

On 18th May, the eve of the 156th anniversary of the birth of Emperor Nicholas II, a new bust-monument to Russia's last Tsar, was installed and consecrated on the grounds of the Orthodox Cultural Center in the village of Zaplavnoye, Leninsky district, Volgograd region.

The solemn ceremony was attended by the foun-der and head of the Volga-Rast group of compa-nies Igor Vitalievich Kapitanov, philanthropist An-drey Yurievich Morozkin, First Vice President of Gazprombank JSC, as well as guests from Moscow, Saratov, Voronezh and Lubansk.

The opening ceremony began with a solemn pa-rade, led by cadets dressed in ceremonial uni-forms. Pupils of the Cadet Corps, along with local high school students and toddlers of the Orthodox Kindergarten, followed behind the cadets through the square, which was decorated with Russian flags.

New bust-monument of Nicholas II, installed in Zaplavnoye on 18th May 2024

New bust-monument of Nicholas II, installed in St. Petersburg on 19th May 2024

The bust-monument was consecrated by the rector of the St. Nicholas Church in the village of Zaplavnoye, Hieromonk Nikita (Sergeev).

The installation of the bust-monument to Emperor Nicholas II was made possible by the All-Russian Alley of Russian Glory Project, the purpose of which is to perpetuate the memory of notable Russians who glorified the Fatherland and the Orthodox faith.

19th May - St. Petersburg

On 19th May 2024 – the day marking the 156th anniversary of the birth of Emperor Nicholas II – a new bust-monument of him was installed on the grounds of the Military Institute of Physical Culture (VIFK), in St. Petersburg.

The event was part of the celebrations marking the 115th anniversary of the Military Institute of Physical Culture (VIFK). The event was attended by St. Petersburg Governor Alexander Beglov and State Secretary and Deputy Minister of Defense of the Russian Federation Nikolai Pankov, both of whom took part in the unveiling and dedication of the bust-monument of Emperor Nicholas II.

On 17th (O.S. 4th) May 1909, Emperor Nicholas II formally granted the provisional regulations for military sports education, which were the basis for the formation of the current institute. The school opened its doors on 14th (O.S. 1st) October 1909 in St Petersburg as the Main Gymnastics and Fencing School, which reported to the Commander of the Imperial Guard/Commanding General, of the St. Petersburg Military District and whose first cadets were military personnel of the Guards units and personnel of the district.

The Military Institute of Physical Culture is the only

and one of the oldest military educational institutions in Russia, which provides training and retraining of specialists in the field of physical culture and sports for ministries and departments of the Russian Federation.

In his dedication speech, Governor Alexander Beglov noted: "Nicholas II was the most athletic emperor in Russia's history. He was a passionate tennis player, he enjoyed all forms of phsical activity, such as cycling, hiking, swimming and rowing, he was excellent at shooting, skiing. He supported sports in Russia. By his example, he brought sports and physical activity to the masses. In addition, it was Nicholas II who brought the rules of *ice hockey to Russia. Now it is a national sport and a favorite game of millions of Russians. * Nicholas II enjoyed playing hockey.

"As our President has repeatedly emphasized, continuity is also important in sports. We must not forget our worthy ancestors. The Institute embodies this wish of the President," said Alexander Beglov.

Governor Alexander Beglov further added that the bust of Nicholas II will remind contemporaries of the Tsar's econtribution to the development of sports and sporting societies in Russia, and to the creation of a system of physical training for officers of the Russian army.

***

NOTE: since the fall of the Soviet Union in 1991, more than 100 monuments, busts and memorial plaques to Emperor Nicholas II have been installed in cities, towns and villages across the Russian Federation. In addition, are a number of churches dedicated to him.

ИМПЕРАТОРСКИЙ
МАРШРУТ

The Imperial Route:
In the Footsteps of Nicholas II

by Paul Gilbert

In 2017, the Imperial Route Project was developed by the Elisabeth-Sergius Educational Society Foundation (ESPO), with the support of the Ministry of Culture of the Russian Federation. The implementation of the project was launched in 2018, the year marking the 100th anniversary of the martyrdom of the Emperor Nicholas II, his Family and other members of the Russian Imperial House.

In 2018, the Imperial Route united 10 regions of Russia: St. Petersburg, Moscow, Tyumen, Sverdlovsk, Omsk, Tomsk, Pskov, Kirov and Perm. A year later, another 9 Russian regions expressed their desire to participate in the national historical and cultural tourism project. By 2024, the Imperial Route united 29 regions of the Russian Federation, from St. Petersburg to Vladivostock.

The 29 participating regions include: St. Petersburg and Tsarskoye Selo, Moscow, Pskovn, Kirov, Perm, Omsk, Tomsk, Sverdlovsk [Ekaterinburg], Tyumen [including Tobolsk], Oryol, Kostroma, Kaluga, Crimea, Novgorod, Bryansk, Kazan, Stavropol, Voronezh, Novosibirsk, Kaliningrad, Tula, Rostov, Nizhny Novgorod, Khabarovsk, Primorsky, Irkutsk, Krasnoyarsk and Yaroslavl.

The participating regions signed a trilateral agreement on the development of the Imperial Route Project. The head of the Federal Agency for Tourism of the Russian Federation Zarina Valerievna Doguzova noted that "the Imperial Route will provide a new impetus for the development and preservation of Russia's historical and cultural heritage and the implementation of new educational programs aimed at the continuity of historical memory".

The goal of the Imperial Route Project is to revive the foundations of the historical, cultural and spiritual component of Russia, during the 300 year reign of the Romanov Dynasty. In particular, the route will focus on Russia's last Emperor Nicholas II and his family: their residences, how they lived, places they visited, how they kept their high traditions of piety, etc. The project will also include those members of the Imperial family who were murdered at Alapaevsk, Perm, Petrograd, etc.

The participants of the project, were informed about the stages of the formation of the Imperial Route, the scientific and educational, museum and exhibition work that was carried out by the ESPO Foundation who have worked with historians, ethnographers, and archivists since 2011. The head of the ESPO Foundation Anna Vitalievna Gromova noted that the task of the project is to acquaint both Russians and foreigners with the achievements of the Imperial House of Romanov, between 1613-1917.

ESPO have been closely involved in a series of major projects that reflect the history of Imperial Russia and the Romanov dynasty, including the Museum of the History of the Imperial Orthodox Palestinian Society in Moscow, the Cross-monument at the site of the death of Grand Duke Sergei Alexandrovich in the Kremlin, the Museum of the Family of Emperor Nicholas II in Tobolsk and the Museum of Memory of the Representatives of the Russian Imperial House in Alapaevsk.

One of the main goals of the Imperial Route is the creation of new museums. The next stages of the development of the project cover places which involved visits and pilgrimages by Nicholas II and

his family. Other projects include the revival of estates and residences, such as the Imperial Estate Ilyinskoye-Usovo in the Moscow region, which belonged to the Empress Maria Alexandrovna, and after her death the residence of Grand Duke Sergei Alexandrovich and Grand Duchess Elizabeth Feodorovna, the Grand Duke Konstantin Konstantinovich's estate in Ostashevo near Moscow, the estate of Grand Duke Mikhail Alexandrovich in the village of Lokot, Bryansk Region, places of visits and pilgrimages in the Kaluga region – the revival of the Sergius Skete, created by the Grand Duchess Elizabeth Feodorovnaof the Orthodox Society in memory of her husband Sergei Alexandrovich, who was assassinated in February 1905. The ESPO Foundation together with the Ministry of Culture of the Russian Federation plans to create up to 10 museums and exhibition spaces along the Imperial Route.

Each region is responsible for implementing commemorative signs at sites participating in the Imperial Route Project, and working with local tourism agencies to promote former Imperial residences, museums, exhibitions, churches, etc., that have a historic connection to the Romanovs. *Tour operators from Germany, Italy, France, Serbia have already shown great interest in this new tourism initiative, which will draw more visitors to Russia, those who wish to learn about the last Tsar and members of his family.

*Once the pandemic is behind us, and travel from the West resumes, tour operators will also offer their services to English speaking visitors from the United States, Canada, Australia and Great Britain.

The National Historical and Cultural Tourism Project The Imperial Route provides an opportunity to take a fresh look at Russia's history and introduce the younger generation to the nations' chain of historical events. "We want to preserve the mem-

Chairman of the Elisabeth-Sergius Educational Society Foundation (ESPO) Anna Vitalievna Gromova.

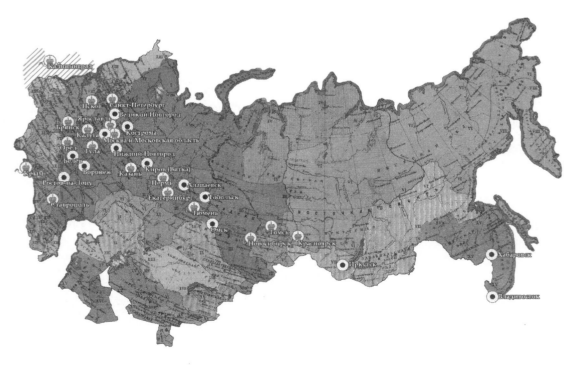

The Imperial Route united 29 regions of the Russian Federation, from St. Petersburg to Vladivostock

The Russian Agency for Tourism promoting the Imperial Route

The Imperial Route train now runs between Tyumen and Tobolsk, as well as Ekaterinburg and Alapaevsk

ory of the 300-year history of Imperial Russia which is famous for its military exploits, scientific achievements, and successes in cultural development. On the Imperial Route everyone will be able to find something of interest, which will not only set examples of the achievements made by members of the Russian Imperial Family, but also to inspire them to live and work for the good of the Fatherland," said Anna Vitalievna Gromova.

In the coming years, the Imperial Route will continue to develop new incentives and places of interest. For instance, on 20th February of this year, a special "Imperial Route" train running between Ekaterinburg and Alapayevsk was launched on the Sverdlovsk Railway (a branch of Russian Railways). The first Imperial Route train was initiated in 2018, between Tyumen and Tobolsk.

This new service is part of the Russian tourist project "Imperial Route," which allows visitors to the Urals to acquaint themselves with places associated with the period – August 1917 to July 1918 – that the Imperial Family were held in Ekaterinburg and Alapaevsk.

The train making the three-hour journey is equipped with an Imperial Family-themed wagon, complete with information boards and video monitors. The train will run on weekends on a special schedule.

Upon arriving in Alapaevsk, visitors are taken by bus to places of importance in the lives of those members of the Imperial Family who were murdered there on 18th July 1918 – the day after Emperor Nicholas II, his family and four faithful retainers were brutally murdered in Ekaterinburg.

In Alapaevsk, 6 members of the Imperial Family, along with 2 faithful servants met a brutal death being thrown down a mineshaft near Alapayevsk by the Bolsheviks. The victims included Grand Duchess Elizabeth Feodorovna, nun Varvara Yakovleva, Grand Duke Sergei Mikhailovich, his secretary Fyodor Remez, Princes of the Imperial Blood Ioann, Konstantin and Igor Konstantinovich and Prince Vladimir Pavlovich Paley.

The goal of the Imperial Route project is to revive the foundations of the historical, cultural and spiritual component of Russia, its achievements during the reign of the Romanov Dynasty.

Revolutionaries burning the Tsar's portrait in 1917. Artist: Ivan Alekseevich Vladimirov (1869-1947)

The myth that Nicholas II's death was met with indifference by the Russian people

by Paul Gilbert

Contemporary historians have led us to believe that news of Nicholas II's death was met with indifference among the Russian people. Rather than conduct their own research on the matter, they choose instead to rehash the popular Bolshevik version of events – this is in itself is not the sign of a good historian.

While the elation exhibited by the revolutionaries is indeed true, it did not reflect the heartfelt senti-

ments of millions of Orthodox Christians, monarchists and others in the former Russian Empire.

Patriarch Tikhon (1865-1925), openly defended the Imperial family, by condemning the Bolsheviks for committing regicide.

When the tragic news of the murder of the Tsar and his family came, the Patriarch immediately served a memorial service at a meeting of the Local Council of the Russian Orthodox Church; then served the funeral Liturgy, saying that no matter how how the Sovereign was judged by his enemies, his murder after he abdicated was an unjustified crime, and those who committed him should be branded as executioners.

During his sermon at the Kazan Cathedral in Moscow, Patriarch Tikhon said:

"... a terrible thing has happened: the former Tsar Nikolai Alexandrovich was shot, by decision of the Ural Regional Soviet of Workers' and Soldiers' Deputies, and our highest government, the Executive Committee, not only approved it but deemed it as legitimate. But our Christian conscience, guided by the Word of God, cannot agree with this. We must, in obedience to the teaching of the Word of God, condemn this act, otherwise the Tsar's blood will fall not just on those who committed it, but on all of us.

"We will not evaluate and judge the deeds of the former Sovereign: an impartial trial of him belongs to history, and now he faces the impartial judgment of God, but we know that he, abdicating the throne, did so with the good of Russia in mind and out of love for the Motherland. He could, after his abdication, have found refuge and lived a quiet life abroad, but he did not do so, choosing to stand with Russia. He did nothing to improve his situation, instead he meekly submitted to fate.

Emperor Nicholas II with Archbishop (future Patriarch) Tikhon
at the Transfiguration Monastery. Yaroslavl, 21 May 1913

Bolshevik thugs went on a campaign of terror and destruction, part of which was to wipe out the memory of Russia's last Tsar and all symbols of monarchy and the Russian Empire.
Artist: Ivan Alekseevich Vladimirov (1869-1947)

"… and suddenly he is sentenced to death somewhere in the depths of Russia, by a small handful of people, not for any guilt, but only for the fact that someone allegedly wanted to kidnap him [the Bolsheviks claimed that the Tsar's family and supporters were attempting to rescue him]…

"Our conscience cannot be reconciled to this, and we must declare it loudly, as Christians, as sons of the church. Let them call us counter-revolutionaries for this, let them imprison us, let them shoot us. We are ready to endure this in the hope that the words of the Savior will be attributed to us: "Blessed are those who hear the Word of God and keep it."

And others condemned the regicide . . .

Eugenie Fraser, born and raised in Russia writes about her years in Petrograd and news of the tsar's death: "In August, filtered through from Siberia, came the news of the slaughter of the Royal family by the sadistic thugs of the Bolshevik party. Horror and revulsion touched every decent thinking citizen in the town. To execute the Tsar and his wife in this barbaric fashion was bad enough, but to butcher the four young girls and the helpless boy was the work of mindless criminals. In churches people went down on their knees and openly wept as they prayed for the souls of the Tsar and his family."

"Even in all this turmoil and confusion, and even among those with little sympathy for the abdicated tsar, the brief five-line announcement in July 1918 of the execution of Nicholas II and his family in Ekaterinburg caused a terrible shock," writes Serge Schmemann. He further notes "Prince Sergei Golitsyn recalled in his diary how people of all

levels of society wept and prayed, and how he himself, as a nine year old boy, cried night after night in his pillow."

Major-General Sir Alfred Knox further noted in his memoirs: "An old soldier . . . breathed into my ear that the Emperor was a good man, and fond of his people, but was surrounded by traitors."

It is important to recall that it was in the summer of 1918, when Lenin unleashed the first Red Terror. People lived in fear of punishment from the thugs and criminals of the new order, for showing any sympathy for the murdered tsar. Many hid their framed portraits of the tsar, and kept their grief and monarchist sentiments to themselves.

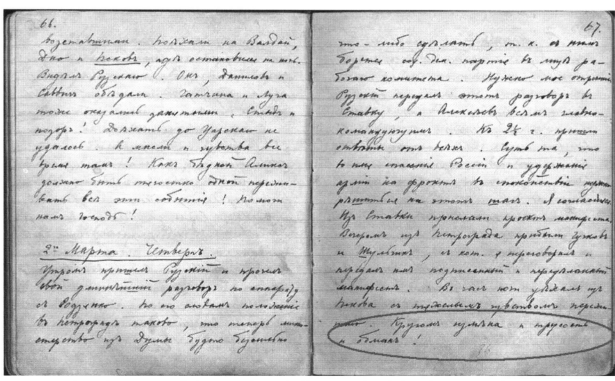

Diary of Emperor Nicholas II - at the end of his entry dated Thursday 2nd March 1917 . . .
«Кругом измена и трусость и обман!»
"All around is betrayal and cowardice and deceit!"

The Poklevsky-Kozell House Museum of the Sverdlovsk Regional Museum of Local Lore in Ekaterinburg

The Romanovs in the Urals
Ekaterinburg

by Paul Gilbert

On 14th July 2023 a new permanent exhibition The Romanovs in the Urals opened at the Poklevsky-Kozell House Museum of the Sverdlovsk Regional Museum of Local Lore in Ekaterinburg.

The exhibition is timed to the 105th anniversary of the death and martyrdom of Emperor Nicholas II and his family in the Ural city on 17th July 1918, and the events marking the 300th anniversary of the founding of Ekaterinburg in 1723.

The exhibit was recently transferred from the Romanov Memorial Hall of the Museum of History and Archaeology of the Urals, and now occupies five newly renovated halls of the Poklevsky-Kozell

House Museum, which is situated at Ulitsa Malysheva, 46. The museum previously hosted the exhibition The Tragedy of the Family ... The Tragedy of the Motherland, which ran from 5th June to 23rd September 2018.

Finishing touches on the new exhibition space were carried out right up until the day before the grand opening. The newly renovated halls smelled of fresh paint, specialists fine tuned the multimedia equipment, caretakers brought shine to the display cases and windows, while researchers installed the last of the exhibits. Their activity aroused the curiosity of both museum workers and visitors, who peeked through the partially open door with the hope of get a glimpse of the Ural city's latest exhibit.

Scientists, researchers, museum workers from across Russia, including Moscow, St. Petersburg, Perm, Tyumen, Tobolsk, Vologda, Voronezh, Ekaterinburg, and Alapaevsk gathered to discuss and help set up the exhibit which features hundreds of items.

The idea to move the Romanov Memorial Hall was proposed by the Chairman of the Elisabeth-Sergius Educational Society Foundation (ESPO) Anna Vitalievna Gromova, who is a Candidate of Historical Sciences, and Senior Researcher at the Institute of World History of the Russian Academy of Sciences.

Anna Gromova is recognized as one of the Russia's most prominent adherents to keeping the memories of Emperor Nicholas II, his family, Grand Duchess Elizabeth Feodorovna, and other members of the Russian Imperial Family who were murdered by the Bolsheviks in 1918 and 1919. She is responsible for the founding and development of museums, exhibitions and conferences and is the mastermind behind the The Imperial Route.

Upon entering the Poklevsky-Kozell House Museum, visitors ascend a newly renovated grand staircase, where they are greeted at the top by

View of the Romanov Memorial Hall in the Museum of History and Archaeology of the Urals. The collection was moved to the Poklevsky-Kozell House Museum, both of which are branches of the Sverdlovsk Regional Museum of Local Lore in Ekaterinburg

portraits of Peter the Great and Emperor Nicholas II. Recall that Ekaterinburg was founded on 18th November 1723 and named after Peter the Great's wife, who after his death became Empress Catherine I, Yekaterina being the Russian form of her name. Underneath the portraits is a miniature copy of Zurab Tsereteli's sculpture, "Night at the Ipatiev House" – the original is on display at the Zurab Tsereteli Museum in Moscow.

The five halls are decorated in the colours of the flag of the Imperial House of Romanov – black, gold, white. Each hall is decorated with unique exhibits and multimedia technologies, which together help to tell the story of the history of the dynasty in the Urals.

In the Golden Hall, are portraits from the era of the chairman of the State Council of the Russian Empire Grand Duke Mikhail Nikolaevich (1832-1909). The highly respected grand duke also served as the Honourary President of the Siberian-Ural Scientific and Industrial Exhibition in 1887, organized on the initiative of the Ural Society of Natural History Lovers (UOLE). When the members of the UOLE created a museum (from which the regional local history traces its history), his son Grand Duke Nikolai Mikhailovich (1859-1909), a famous Russian historian, became its patron. At the turn of the 20th century, six additional members of Russian Imperial House were made honourary members of the UOLE.

The "black" halls of the exhibit take on a more sombre ambiance, with displays telling visitors about the house arrest and subsequent murders of Grand Duke Mikhail Alexandrovich and Nicholas Johnson at Perm on 13th June 1918; Emperor Nicholas II, his family and four faithful retainers at Ekaterinburg on 17th July 1918; and Grand Duchess Elizabeth Feodorovna along with and other members of the Russian Imperial Family and their faithful retainers at Alapaevsk on 18th July 1918.

Some of the more interesting items on display include the ribbon of the Order of St. Andrew the First-Called, which belonged to Tsesarevich Alexei Nikolaevich and left behind in the Governor's Mansion in Tobolsk, when the four children joined their parents and sister in Ekaterinburg in May 1918.

A number of pistols and revolvers are also on display, including the Mauser of the regicide Pyotr [Peter] Ermakov, who, according to him, shot and killed Nicholas II.

The sombre ambiance of this hall is offset by the bright and soothing icon of the Holy Royal Martyrs, painted by the nuns of the Novo-Tikhvin Convent in Ekaterinburg.

The Romanovs in the Urals also contains many elements of décor, decoration and fittings salvaged from the Ipatiev House before its demolition in September 1977, notably the cast iron fireplace from the dining room, and the iron grille from the window of the murder room.

Aside from the items from the Ipatiev House, are many additional exhibits of interest, including a scale model of the Ipatiev House; the reconstructed model of Nicholas II's head by Russian forensic expert Dr. Sergei Nikitin.

The exposition further explores the history of the investigation of the murder case of the last of the Romanovs in the Urals, which lasted more than 100 years.

Portraits of Peter the Great and Nicholas II are the centerpiece of the staircase leading to the exhibition

Miniature copy of Zurab Tsereteli's sculpture, "Night at the Ipatiev House" on display on the staircase

The original cast iron fireplace, salvaged from the dining room of the Ipatiev House in September 1977

Revolvers used by the regicides to murder the Imperial Family in the Ipatiev House on 17th July 1918

An icon of the Holy Royal Martyrs, painted by the nuns of the Novo-Tikhvin Convent in Ekaterinburg

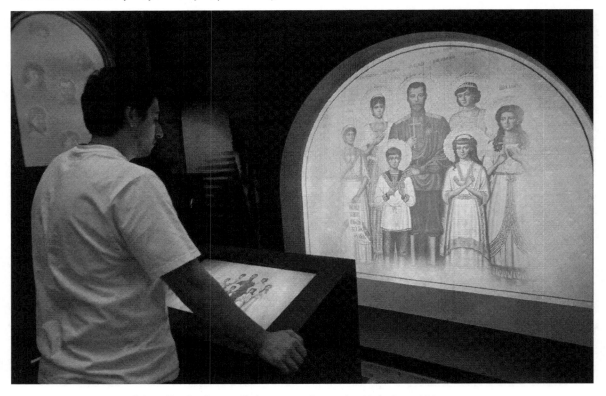

Multimedia displays tell the story about the Holy Royal Martyrs

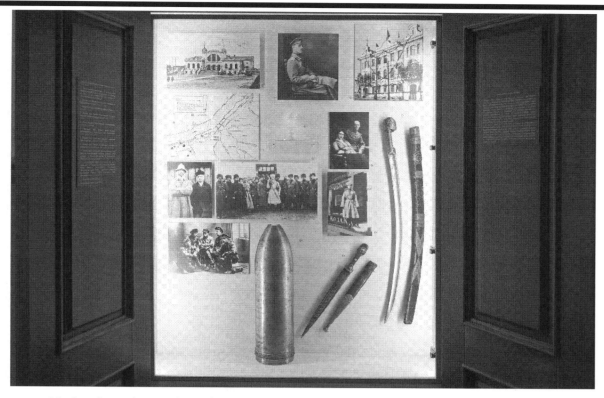

Display about the murders of Grand Duke Mikhail Alexandrovich at Perm on 13th June 1918

Display about the murders of members of the Imperial Family at Alapaevsk on 18th July 1918

Putin's negative assessment of Nicholas II

by Paul Gilbert

During his presidency, Vladimir Putin has spoken negatively about Nicholas II on more than one occasion, describing his role as a ruler "erroneous" and "absurd". Putin believes that Nicholas II ruled the country incorrectly, made many mistakes, which is why Russia lost the Russo-Japanese War (1904-05) and later lead Russia unprepared into the First World War. Putin further believes that during the war, Nicholas II personally made a number of errors of judgment and policy, which forced his highest ranking military officers to seek his removal from the throne by forcing the Tsar to abdicate. The main conspirators were mainly military

leaders and self-serving politicians of the Duma.

Vladimir Putin has also publicly referred to Russia's last tsar as "Bloody Nicholas" on more than one occasion. His negative attitude towards Nicholas II, however, does not reflect his assessment of other Russian monarchs, including the Emperors Peter I, Nicholas I, Alexander II, and Alexander III.

"Nicholas the Bloody"

A video has been circulating on YouTube for some years now, in which Putin is caught on camera making an insult towards Nicholas II. Entering his Kremlin office (probably on the day of his first inauguration on 7th May 2000), Putin responds to these words spoken by one of his aides: "From this roof [Grand Kremlin Palace], Nicholas II looked out over Moscow."

"Well, he had nothing to do, so he ran across the roofs," Russia's new President remarked contemptuously.

During a meeting with members of construction teams in Sochi in the summer of 2011, Putin referred to the Tsar as "Nicholas the Bloody". This epithet runs counter to both the position of the Russian Orthodox Church, which canonized Nicholas II on 20th August 2000, and with the ideology of the Russian authorities during the past 20 years.

Then, on 4th March 2014, during a press conference in Novo-Ogaryov on the events in Ukraine and the annexation of Crimea, Vladimir Putin once again, used the Soviet propaganda epithet "Nicholas the Bloody". He was responding to a question by a journalist of the Interfax news agency, Putin said the following: "A simple Ukrainian citizen, a Ukrainian man suffered both under Nicholas the Bloody and under [Leonid] Kravchuk …".

Then again, on 15th March 2014, the day marking the anniversary of the bloody February coup of 1917, in which Emperor Nicholas II was forcibly removed from the throne, and who accepted a martyr's crown on 17th July 1918, Putin during a press conference boorishly insulted the popularly revered Tsar-Martyr, referring to him as "Nicholas the Bloody".

In 2016, Putin visited an exhibition dedicated to the 150th anniversary of the artist Valentin Serov, held at the State Tretyakov Gallery in Moscow. He was photographed admiring Serov's iconic portrait of Emperor Nicholas II (1900).

Why is Putin negative about Nicholas II?

Vladimir Putin probably has a negative attitude towards Nicholas II, because he grew up in Soviet times, where, in principle, Nicholas II was presented as an unambiguously negative character, who refused to progress and generally failed any undertakings. It was during the Soviet years, that Russia's last tsar was more often than not, referred to as "Bloody Nicholas" – old habits die hard.

During the Stalin era, documents and photographs which depicted the last tsar were seized and destroyed, as they were deemed as "ideologically harmful". It was Joseph Stalin who ordered the Romanov archives closed and sealed. They were even off limits to historians, unless for propaganda purposes. Up until the fall of the Soviet Union in 1991, these private documents and photographs effectively lay untouched.

Russian historian Pyotr Multatuli notes: "Stalin forbade any mentioning of the hideous crime in Ekaterinburg, because he was well aware that it was working against his regime.

"Stalin, too, was building his empire, but it was an empire that did not have anything in common with the Russian Empire. Stalin's empire did not pursue the interests of the Russian people. What was the nature of the Russian monarchy? There was God, the Tsar as the father of the people, and the people were his children, whom he loved, but whom he could also punish."

Perhaps the key to unravelling Putin's negative attitude towards Nicholas II lies in his words, spoken during a press conference on 22nd December 2010, when Putin served as Prime Minister of Russia under President Dmitry Medvedev:

"And, frankly speaking, he was not an important politician. Otherwise, the empire would have survived. Although this is not only his fault."

Putin believes, that Nicholas II, as an autocrat, bears the main responsibility for what happened during his 22+ year reign, which resulted in the collapse of both the monarchy and the Russian Empire.

Putin is the only top Russian official who speaks out negatively against Nicholas II. The rest of the top officials, for example Prime Minister Dmitry Medvedev, and Russia's former Minister of Culture Vladimir Medinsky, have both only spoken positively about the last Tsar.

The Russian clergy evaluate Putin's epithet

Putin's criticisms of Nicholas II have offended both Orthodox Christians and monarchists over the years, however, Archpriest Valery Rozhnov of the Russian Orthodox Church Outside Russia (ROCOR), issued the following statement dated 7th March 2014:

"Since the words of the president in Russian political culture are often perceived as political truth, the phrase about the "Nicholas the Bloody" can have far-reaching consequences.

"As you know, the epithet was part of Soviet propaganda, which was based on many human lives during the reign of the last Russian emperor. However, after the collapse of the USSR, the rhetoric changed, and Nicholas II began to be presented as a victim of circumstances and a tragic figure. It was only when the Russian Orthodox Church canonized the tsar as a saint, that the authorities began to reassess Nicholas II. President Boris Yeltsin, for example, even participated in the

A magnificent giled bowsprint in the shape of a double-headed eagle
lunged forward from the bow of the Imperial Yacht *Standart*

burial of the tsar's remains in the Peter and Paul Cathedral [17th July 1998].

"Through Putin's words, Soviet rhetoric once again returned to official discourse. This can have serious consequences both for the Russian Orthodox Church and for Ekaterinburg, where Nicholas II became a figure of meaning. Ekaterinburg as a place of the execution of the royal family and a place of repentance for this crime has become a center of pilgrimage and tourism. There is a monument to the imperial family in the city; a church and a monastery were built in their honour. If Nicholas II is again declared "Bloody" and not saint, then this entire industry may be called into question.

"Whether the phrase dropped by Putin is yet another sign of the return of Soviet propaganda clichés, or is this just his personal opinion, which does not claim any ideological status, the position will become clear in the future. In particular, the rhetoric of Russian officials in relation to Nicholas II and tsarist Russia in general will be of particular interest, especially given the century since the beginning of the First World War."
Putin denounces Lenin for murder of Nicholas II

Since Putin's rise to power, the head of the Russian Orthodox Church has proclaimed the last tsar, his wife and children, as saints, which was viewed with fear in a country where the Imperial family are still victims of a century of myths and lies, much of which are based on Bolshevik propaganda. In addition to canonization, the Church also decided to build a grand church on the site where the family was murdered in Ekaterinburg on 17th July 1918. In 2003, during a visit to the Urals, President Putin visited the Church on the Blood in Ekaterinburg.

Despite the negative comments made by Putin, he has also made a number of positive gestures regarding Nicholas II, which left many people surprised. During a state visit to France in 2008, Putin visited the Museum of His Majesty's Lifeguards Cossack Regiment in Courbevoie, where he posed in front of a portrait of the tsar.

On 25th January 2016, while speaking at an interregional forum of the All-Russia People's Front, Vladimir Putin denounced Bolshevik leader Vladimir Lenin, for "brutally executing Russia's last Tsar along with all his family and servants". Putin further criticized Lenin, accusing him of placing a "time bomb" under the state, and sharply denouncing brutal repressions by the Bolshevik government, murdering thousands of priests and innocent civilians.

In the weeks leasing up to the 100th anniversary of the death and martyrdom of Nicholas II, rumours in the Russian media speculated that Putin would attend the Patriarchal Liturgy, to be performed by His Holiness Patriarch Kirill on the night of 16/17 July 2018. Sadly, this was not to be, instead, he flew to Helsinki, where he met with US president Donald Trump. More than 100,000 people from across Russia and around the world descended on the Ural capital to honour the memory of the Holy Royal Martyrs.

Putin's presence on the eve of the centenary, would have indeed been an historic event, one which perhaps would further seal post-Soviet Russia's condemnation of the Bolsheviks for committing regicide, but also shedding the century of myths and lies, which perpetuated during the Soviet years.

Sadly, the 100th anniversary of the Romanovs' deaths passed with little notice in Russia. The Russian government ignored the anniversary, as it surprisingly did the year before, when Russia marked

On 17th July 2019, members of the State Duma for the first time in history, observed a minute of silence in memory of the last Russian emperor Nicholas II, and all those killed in the Civil War (1917-1922)

the 100th anniversary of the 1917 October Revolution. No prominent state museums or venues hosted events to mark the anniversary. The few exhibitions and other events organized were tellingly modest.

On a more positive note, on 17th July 2019 – Russia's State Duma for the first time observed a minute of silence in memory of the last Russian emperor Nicholas II and all those killed in the Civil War. (1917-1922)

According to Duma Speaker Vyacheslav Volodin, "reconciliation begins when we all understand that this cannot be repeated and this is unacceptable."

"Today we are making a proposal to honour the memory of the last Russian tsar, to honour the memory of the innocent victims – all those who died in the crucible of the Civil War," the speaker addressed his colleagues, who after these words, rose from their seats.

It should come as no surprise that members of the Communist Party of the Russian Federation, did not comply with the moment of silence.

The fact that this is the first time in the history of Russia's State Duma, that they honoured the memory of Nicholas II is truly unprecedented! The minute of silence was repeated in 2020 and will be repeated each year from hereon.

Also, in 2019, Russian media reported that Putin had urged the Russian Orthodox Church to "reach a verdict soon" on the Ekaterinburg Remains.

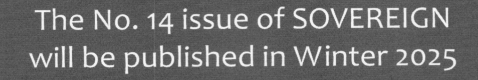

The No. 14 issue of SOVEREIGN
will be published in Winter 2025

SOVEREIGN

THE LIFE AND REIGN OF EMPEROR NICHOLAS II

No. 14   2025

PAUL GILBERT

NICHOLAS II

EMPEROR. TSAR. SAINT.

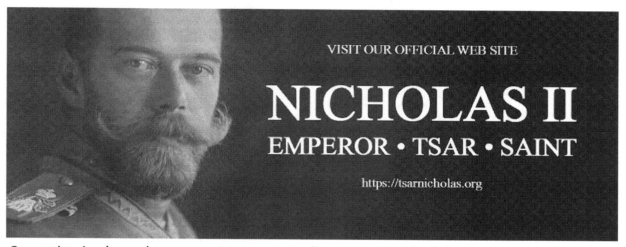

Sovereign is pleased to present two new online resources for information on Nicholas II. Both resources will feature articles, news stories (translated from Russian media sources), videos, photos, book reviews, and more.

Like our semi-annual journal Sovereign, the new web site and Facebook pages, are dedicated to clearing the name of Russia's much slandered emperor and tsar, giving voice to post-Soviet Russian historians, who are committed to rewriting the history of Russia's most misunderstood and maligned ruler.

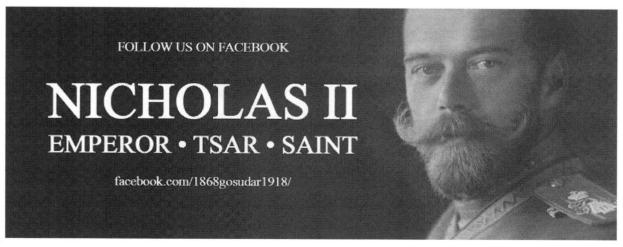

The Nicholas II web and Facebook pages are maintained by Sovereign, and its' editor and publisher Paul Gilbert

NICHOLAS II

EMPEROR · TSAR · SAINT

*Dedicated to clearing the name of
Russia's much slandered Tsar*

tsarnicholas.org

Made in the USA
Middletown, DE
18 June 2024